Developing Independent Learning in Science

D1584483

Developing Independent Learning in Science

Practical Ideas and Activities for 7–12-year-olds

Liz Lakin

Open University Press

Open University Press
McGraw-Hill Education
McGraw-Hill House
Shoppenhangers Road
Maidenhead
Berkshire
England
SL6 2QL

email: enquiries@openup.co.uk
world wide web: www.openup.co.uk

and Two Penn Plaza, New York, NY 10121–2289, USA

First published 2013

A catalogue record of this book is available from the British Library

ISBN-13: 978-0-33-524620-5 (pb)
ISBN-10: 0-33-524620-6 (pb)
eISBN: 978-0-33-524621-2

Library of Congress Cataloging-in-Publication Data
CIP data applied for

Typesetting and e-book compilations by
RefineCatch Limited, Bungay, Suffolk

Praise for this book

"A truly-thought provoking, interactive book with a difference that takes teachers on a learning journey. It encourages us to reflect on how we learn, how our pupils learn and what the collective implications for effective teaching and helping pupils to construct their learning are.

Reading and actively engaging with this book is indeed a learning journey, invaluable to practitioners. The text contains many invaluable references and deals with topics such as the value of homework, how people learn and how people respond to techniques addressee to hem in learning situations.

An essential reading for practicing teachers and particularly students in training and their tutors."

Dr Sue Dale Tunnicliffe, Senior lecturer in Science Education,
Institute of Education, University of London, UK

"There has never been a time when independent learning is more important in school science. In Developing Independent Learning in Science, Liz Lakin challenges the reader to examine how they teach science and why pupils respond as they do. The result is a book that should be of great value to those who teach science to 7-12 year-olds and to science educators in general. A particular strength is the way the author interweaves rigorous thinking about learning with activities for the reader to help them engage with the text. In addition, there is a mass of useful thinking in here and plenty of classroom suggestions. The book is worth reading simply for the honesty of the 'How not to climb Helvellyn' case study."

Michael J Reiss, Professor of Science Education,
Institute of Education, University of London, UK

"In this book Liz Lakin involves the readers in the kind of independent learning that she in describing and advocating. It should enable practising teachers to stand back from their work to consider why we want children to learn in a certain way as well as providing useful ideas about how to do it. It is written in a personal and engaging style and is a unique addition to books on science teaching."

Wynne Harlen, OBE, PhD. Visiting Professor of Education,
University of Bristol, UK

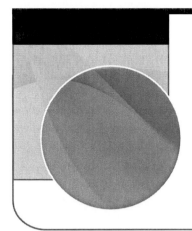

Contents

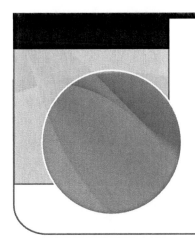

Acknowledgements

My thanks and appreciation go to George Burch for his attention to detail both pedagogically and typographically throughout this book and to Colin Forster for bringing his expertise on 'homework' to the final chapter. More significantly though, to the many teachers, trainee teachers and pupils who over the years have contributed to the materials and scenarios that informed the contents of this book, my thanks go to you all.

Cover picture: Environment Matters

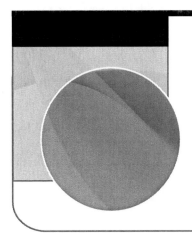

Introduction

This is a book about teaching and learning in science education, but what makes it different from other such texts is that it challenges you, the reader, to really engage with and constructively analyse the learning process: to consider why you teach something in the way you do, why your pupils respond in the way they do and what are the collective implications of the instructions and actions carried out.

This book aims to raise standards by providing opportunities for pupils to develop as independent learners. To achieve this we gain greater insight into the learning process by examining, as teachers, our own learning and that of our pupils, thereby informing and developing our practice in the classroom.

This book takes you on a 'learning journey' that begins by investigating how we learn and applying this to science education. Throughout the first two chapters time is spend introducing and exploring the concept of 'independent learning'. This exploration unfolds in Chapters 3 and 4 as a range of existing strategies, based on current educational research, are developed and analysed within the primary and early secondary classroom. Chapter 5 further expands the theme of independent learning through the use of problem-solving and the establishment of a learning community. By Chapter 6 the learning journey takes us beyond the classroom setting and the confines of school-based learning using 'homework' as the vehicle. Central to the successful outcome of the journey are you, the teacher, your pupils and others engaged in the learning process; collectively you will all determine the nature and quality of that outcome.

Underpinning the journey's focus are several key ideas that feature throughout the book. Individually they are important to effective learning in their own right; collectively, however, they add a dimension to learning and teaching that can truly empower the learner. Not only do they enable the learner to take responsibility for their own learning but by encouraging the use of these skills and ideas, pupils can re-examine their thoughts, identifying what they know and how they know it and question assumptions made and clarifications required, while recognizing what they must do next to progress and develop their understanding further. In short, they become autonomous and creative in their thinking and constructively critical of their understanding. Pupils who have developed and readily use these skills have become truly independent in their learning. The ideas and skills that permeate through this learning journey are to:

- focus on the 'big picture' as well as the minutia;
- apply learning theory and an understanding of how we learn;
- encourage the effective use of learning outcomes and related assessment;
- recognize alternative ideas and ways of seeing things;
- recognize the role of problem-based and enquiry-based learning in the learning process, and encourage the use of informed and 'rich' questions that tease out deeper understanding.

For these skills and ideas to be effective, they must be practised and honed. Learners must be allowed opportunities to reformulate their thinking and 'test' out their ideas by explaining and discussing them with others. It is here that the social aspect of learning and thus 'interdependent learning' become so important. This final underlying principle concerns the development of a 'learning community' within which learners develop as individuals and collectively as part of the community. Such safe, non-threatening working environments are fundamental to any learning process but crucial in allowing autonomous learning to develop through the use of constructive questioning and problem-solving. As teachers, this is something we strive to achieve. The strategies, scenarios and activities presented throughout this learning journey here in this book will, with careful adaptation and application, help ideals become realities.

CHAPTER 1

Independent learning: what is it and why is it important?

'Give a man a fish and you feed him for a day, teach him how to fish and you feed him for a lifetime'.

(Chinese proverb)

Introduction

With an emphasis on the learner being central to any learning process, this introductory chapter sets the tone for the book. It is essential that you and your pupils (in the role of learners) are central to this book. So I begin by drawing attention to your *learning*; what you consider it is and how you perceive the learning process. I go on to challenge you to reflect on the process you undertake when learning something new. I then explore different types of learning, thinking about the disparity between 'shallow' and 'deep' learning. With this in mind I introduce the idea of 'independent learning' and explore its various perspectives and the different views people hold about this term. Through a series of activities and examples, I suggest how autonomous, creative and critically reflective learning can be introduced and developed. Future chapters in the book pick up the reins of development presenting ideas, strategies and suggestions, while emphasizing the unique role middle-phase education (7–12-year-olds) has to play in the process.

As you progress through this chapter bear in mind how you learn and consider why you do things in the way you do: what influences affect *you* as a learner and the learning process you undertake? What are the likely implications and impact of the subsequent actions you perform and do they enhance or hinder the learning process overall?

> **Key ideas in this chapter:** Independent learning in its various guises; deep and shallow learning; impact and implications of independent learning.

What is learning and how do we do it?

> ### Activity 1.1 Thinking about learning (I)
>
> Consider for a moment what you understand by the verb 'to learn'. How do you know when you have learnt something and how does that learning take place?
>
> To externalize your thoughts, jot them down in a notebook or share them with a colleague.

The word 'learn' comes from the old English term *lore*, as in *farming lore*, which literally means 'instruction' and refers to a body of traditions and knowledge on a subject, in this case farming. Perceiving the term in this way reinforces the idea of 'imparting information' to a previously information-less being. We know from Ausubel (1968) and others that learners of all ages and types are not blank canvases on which to impart information. They can be influenced, yes, but every learner brings with them to the learning situation their unique perception of the world from their previous experiences. We forget this at our peril! This important issue is revisited in Chapter 2.

From a theoretical educator's point of view Kyriacou (2001) describes learning as a person's changes in behaviour that takes place as a result of being engaged in an educational experience. This suggests the capacity to do something different from what could be done before. How does this equate with your own perception of 'learning'?

> ### Activity 1.2   Thinking about learning (II)
>
> Now consider how you learn something new. Begin with something that naturally interests you; for example, a new language for your

holidays, a new dance routine, a new swimming stroke, or learning to use a new piece of technology.

How do you set about achieving this? Record your thoughts as a flow diagram.

As we reflect on our learning we realize that we approach learning in different ways. The approach used, the motivators and the amount of time we dedicate to the process may vary considerably. An example of this comes from some undergraduate students discussing motivation and learning. Having initially discussed why and how they learn, they debate some of the issues they encounter and the demotivation they sometimes experience, especially when learning certain topics. As the dialogue develops they stumble over an example of learning for learning's sake; in this quote the student is referring to learning to play the guitar, purely for pleasure . . . 'You decide to learn it and you learn it. You know, it's not because someone says you've got to learn guitar.' This was immensely rewarding to hear, especially considering the beginning of the diatribe went something like this:

> . . . You know, I've learnt because I need to learn for assignments . . . I've quite enjoyed it sometimes, but I can't think when I've ever been to the library and thought, ooh, I want to learn about such and such today, I'm going to get a book out and learn about it.
>
> *(BSc QTS Year 2 student, 2009)*

Think about how this relates to you: I can certainly find plenty of displacement activities to do instead of focusing on the work I know I should be doing. The outcomes arising from such a situation where we learn something *because we have to* is that the information has little meaning or 'depth', and may be easily forgotten.

Activity 1.3 Thinking about 'shallow' learning

The last time you sat an exam or took a test, for example, your driving test, how much of the detail you imparted during the test can you recall now?

How much do you think you could recall immediately after the exam?

Often the reply to this is '... not very much!' This is because the information was only committed to the short-term memory, never being fully embedded in the longer term.

This is an example of 'shallow' learning and is typified by cramming for an exam.

For the learning process to be productive the learner must first take ownership of the ideas. Until this happens the learner's engagement remains superficial, and 'deep learning', the type that is sustained, which can be applied to new situations and further developed, remains beyond their grasp. To achieve this demands an inner drive or motivation that arises from the learner themselves. The information must have relevance and be accessible to the learner, but more importantly the learner must *want* to learn it. It is this final prerequisite that is so fundamental to any learning process: without that motivation, without that innermost drive, learning becomes a mundane, meaningless operation fit only for an objective-driven assessment process.

Consider the following activity:

Activity 1.4 Non-contextualized teaching

Using the information provided, calculate the distance between A and D using the following routes and decide which is the shortest route, calling at all points and why.

A to B = 5 km

B to C = 3 km

B to D = 6 km

C to D = 10 km

Alternative routes:

(1)   A to B to C to D   5 + 3 + 10 = 18 km

(2)   A to B to C to B to D   5 + 3 + 3 + 6 = 17 km

Answer = Route 2 because it is shorter by 1 km

'...but I *wanted* to pass my driving test' I hear you exclaim! And I wanted to pass my French CSE which I got such an abysmal grade for considering I was taught it and tried to learn it for nine years. So where did it all go wrong? This I believe is where our approach to primary education and its underpinning research and developmental strategies play such a unique and significant role.

Now consider the same problem but set in a familiar context.

Activity 1.5 Contextualized teaching

It was Christmas Eve and Father Christmas had three final stops to make before he could give the reindeers a break at a special hideaway lodge in the forest. He was rather concerned because Dasher, one of his most reliable reindeers, had knocked his hind leg and really needed that rest. Father Christmas had three more houses to visit on the way but he must decide which would be the shortest route to take to get him to the lodge as quickly as possible. Using the information below, can you help Father Christmas decide which route would be the shortest and by how much?

- Jonny Granger's house to The Old House on the Hill is 5 km
- The Old House on the Hill to Little Sally Mathis' house is 3 km
- The Old House on the Hill straight to the Lodge is 6 km and,
- Little Sally Mathis' house to the Lodge is 10 km.

The calculation is exactly the same as the example in Activity 1.4. By placing the problem in a recognizable context it gives meaning to the seemly inexplicable; that is, why C (Little Sally Mathis' house) should be included in the calculation. It also, of course, makes the exercise more interesting. One argument against this approach is that it could make the whole thing more complicated; this of course would be more challenging and could be made more accessible by drawing a map and including pictures to illustrate the information!

The same argument of course applies to primary science, having no obvious relevance other than the concept or idea we are trying to demonstrate at the time. Instead we set the scene for our investigation aiming to capture the pupils' imagination and hopefully drawing them into the challenge of the investigation by giving them ownership over the exercise. This way the learner indeed becomes central to the learning process, but is this what we mean by *independent learning*?

Independent learning: what exactly is it?

To answer this question we must first examine what went wrong in the above situation concerning my learning of French. I suspect the problem with the way I tried to learn French some 30 years ago and why I can only remember snippets, such as counting to 10 and survival phrases such as 'Parlez vous Anglais?', was to do with the way it was taught. In those days language tuition was not set in a *cultural* context; there was little inspiration attached to it despite attempts to set the exercises within a familiar context and the innovative use of a 'language lab' using technology that emphasized individual learning through audio input and repetition. Owing to the nature of the technology it was possible for the teacher to listen to us individually. The idea was ground-breaking at the time but for me the lessons lacked the opportunity to develop any real understanding of the language. I was essentially cramming for an exam, learning the content to pass a specific test, and forgetting the majority of it as soon as I walked out of the exam hall; a classic example of shallow learning. The end product, any 'knowledge' I did retain, was disconnected from reality, only useful in very specific situations; it lacked depth and real understanding on my part. Biggs and Tang (2009) describe this type of learning as characterized by an intention only to complete the task requirements, usually by memorizing information for assessment purposes while often associating facts and concepts unreflectively. Significant emphasis, as we have seen, is placed on external or extrinsic drivers, such as passing the examination.

From a pedagogic standing this type of learning and the modes of teaching that promote it have been demonstrated to lead in the long term to pupils' reduced confidence, demotivation and subsequent strategic, assessment-oriented approach to learning (Lakin, 2010). *Deep learning*, on the other hand, is characterized by an intention to 'understand' and has an internal, intrinsic motivational emphasis. It requires the acquisition of specific higher-order problem-solving skills, such as those of analysis, interpretation and evaluating: we return to the acquisition of these specific skills in Chapter 3, 4 and 5.

The idea that deep learning is internally motivated suggests a degree of ownership on the part of the learner. As teachers we recognize this as being an important factor in encouraging engagement. However, the use of the term 'ownership' does have its limitations: one can be given or assume ownership of something but not do anything about it. The process has to be active and the learner must assume some responsibility for it. Think again about learning a language. It is not just to do with knowing the words, how they are pronounced properly or fit together in a coherent manner. To speak a foreign language you need to know how the language 'works', which relates to culture and emotion. To develop a real under-standing of the 'fabric' of a language takes time, engagement, practice and commitment, all of which demand learner motivation and drive. So where does the teacher feature in all this? We provide the context and opportuni-ties for this type of learning to develop, thereby enabling the learner to assume increasing responsibility for the learning process. For Pritchard (2005) this is what independent learning is all about: learners being given and accepting increasing amounts of responsibility for their own learning.

With this in mind, think about Activity 1.6 that invites you to examine your own perception of independent learning.

Activity 1.6 Examining your own perception of independent learning

First, think about yourself as a learner.

- How do you learn best?
- What do you do and what factors influence your learning process? You need to clarify this concept before moving on.

Now in relation to your class and you as a teacher, answer the following questions:

- How do you perceive the term *independent learning*?
- Compare your view with that of several colleagues.
  - What similarities do they show and what differences?
  - What factors do you think influenced or determined the various answers?
- Do you consider yourself to be an independent learner?

  - Justify your answer whatever it may be.

When a group of teachers of 7–12-year-olds were asked these questions, they presented some interesting similarities in their responses, yet also some very significant differences. For example the term 'ownership' featured in at least a third of the answers although only a third of these mentioned the more active approach of taking responsibility for their learning. Several mentioned that independent learners displayed the higher-level skills of reflection, analysis and evaluation. Others mentioned that such people were able to improve their learning through the use of constructive feedback and at times were capable of self-correction. The majority of the responses referred to working by oneself, without any instruction or teacher input. Again this varied in complexity; some referred merely to working alone, while others recognized that the learner was driving their own learning, making decisions and seeking out information with minimal guidance and support. Some responses commented on the benefits afforded by peers and other people involved in supporting the independent learner; they were essentially talking about the credentials of a learning community. A summary of these responses and the spectrum across which they spanned is included in Table 1.1.

Teachers' perception of the term 'independent learning'

These responses go some way towards an accepted definition for 'independent learning' that has developed over several years of research and pedagogic application:

> the ability [of the learner] to assess their own knowledge and understanding in the light of information received, and if necessary, self-correct and direct progression in relation to their reflectively perceived needs. To achieve this, the learner must be autonomous and creative in their thinking and constructively critical of their understanding.
>
> (Lakin, 2010:7)

So what does this mean, how does it relate to you as a teacher of pupils between the years of 7 and 12, and why is it so important? The responses summarized in Table 1.1 collectively provide a good explanation of what independent learning is all about. Clearly it goes beyond working in physical isolation. In fact it has been stated that perhaps a better term would be 'interdependent learning' (Lakin, 2010) because this type of learning so often involves influence, discussion and debate from others including parents, grandparents, teachers, peers and so on. Independent learning has rather candidly been described as the 'Martini approach' to

Table 1.1 Teachers' views on independent learning

Characteristic	Spectrum of examples			
	Assuming ownership – passive	Assuming responsibility – Guided and facilitated by HoS	Demonstrating autonomy	Demonstrating reflective and analytical practice
Approaches to learning		Able to follow instruction	Demonstrate an enthusiasm for learning	Aware of how to learn leading to deeper knowledge and understanding.
Able to improve a task – can act on feedback	Using feedback to amend/improve their work	Self-assessing	Self/peer-assessing and providing constructive feedback	Able to self-correct and improve their performance
Make own choices e.g. equipment, resources, etc.	With support			Autonomously
Finding information for themselves/ knowing how to find out more	Able to pose their own questions	Know where to look	Know how to find information	Able to assess effectiveness of research process

(continued overleaf)

Table 1.1 continued

Characteristic	Spectrum of examples			
Directed/managed by learner Partly or solely	Work with some direction	Ask teacher using own initiative	Direct their own learning	Manage and direct their own learning
Allow to work at own pace but teacher-directed Actively learning	Teacher directed – able to be flexible with timing	Providing active learning activities	Providing graded resources and extension work	
Learning community	Input from teacher and pupils	Work within a pre-established working group	Recognize school as a learning community	Wider learning community Including parents, etc.
Works on own without help or structured direction	Work on own but with some direction	Pupil-led	Direct their own learning	Self-correct

learning: anytime, anyplace, anywhere, with anyone! This is because 'independent learning' is a process that the learner goes through themselves – it isn't something that can be done to them; they can be influenced, guided and supported by others but this in-depth learning they have to do themselves. They are the one making the decisions, directing and managing the process, reflecting on progress, seeking out new information and applying it where necessary. During this procedure they are constructing meaning and developing understanding – they are *independent learners*. This of course is the ultimate goal, the panacea to the woes of higher education which cries out for students with these transferable, higher-order 'employability' skills that are reportedly missing from the recruitment market.

If this is the case and the independent learner is truly autonomous, then what is our role as teachers? First we must remember that becoming an independent learner is something that develops over time; we must, therefore, consider the full education spectrum and recognize that this age range (7–12) is one part of the whole spectrum. Second, as professional practitioners we aim to guide, scaffold, facilitate and enable learning by providing suitably differentiated learning opportunities for our pupils. These are all qualities that go towards promoting independent learning. So you are probably doing it anyway ... consider Activity 1.7.

Activity 1.7 Examining your own practice

Think about your class and answer the following questions:

- What opportunities have you given your pupils over the past week that allows them to take responsibility for their learning?
- How did they respond? Identify a pupil who you feel is or aspires to being an independent learner and one pupil who you feel finds this more challenging.
- List the evidence you have to support your decision.

It is often helpful to compare and discuss your answers with a colleague, especially someone you feel comfortable talking to and who knows your pupils. Try this and see what their thoughts are.

Some suggestions put forward by other teachers are listed in Table 1.2. They are expounded later in Chapters 3, 4 and 5.

You will probably recognize several of these examples already in your teaching. You will also recognize that not all pupils aspire to them and indeed we should not expect them to. This is where your role features significantly. The two important features here concern differentiation in terms of scope and the quality of guidance:

- Scope – refers to what the pupils are being asked to do, the detail, the depth of understanding, the amount of complexity, the use and evaluation of different approaches, the amount of uncertainty.

- Guidance – how much information and structure pupils will be given and how much they are expected to do using their own initiative.

Table 1.2 Some teachers' responses to examining and promoting independent learning opportunities and where they are addressed in Chapters 3, 4 and 5	

Developing self-esteem
 • Enabling pupils to take responsibility for a particular task in class
   o i.e. book monitor
 • Communicating information
   o pupils plan and give presentations
 • Encouraging flexibility in their approach to things
	Chapter 3

Practising a new skill or newly acquired information and applying it in a new context	Chapter 3
Making use of context and real-life situations	Chapter 3
Focusing on the learning process rather than just the products of learning	Chapters 3 and 4
Connecting new information with previously acquired information	Chapter 4
Encouraging pupils to self-monitor and record achievements	Chapters 3 and 4
Helping, setting and solving each other's problems	Chapter 5
Making reviewing and reflecting on learning a regular feature in lessons	Chapters 4 and 5

It is these features that underpin learning development and progression. If we consider the latter certain stages come to mind; have a go at the example in Activity 1.8:

Independent learning

Activity 1.8 Exploring developmental progression

Complete the following table that summarizes developmental progression from the learner's perspective. The first one is done for you.

Teacher dependent	——▶	Teacher independent
Simple	——▶	
	——▶	Explain
Use everyday language	——▶	
Concrete level of thinking	——▶	
Copy word for word	——▶	

Suggested answers are available at the end of this chapter.

The activity above outlines extremes on different spectra of progression. From a teaching point of view we must be able to differentiate across the progression spectrum. To achieve this we need to consider the varying levels of scope and guidance available to the teacher. For example, we often prompt pupils to explain their descriptive accounts by including the word 'because' on a worksheet or by asking them 'why they *think* such-and-such has occurred'. This will reveal levels of understanding that serve as useful formative feedback. When considering progression from concrete to abstract scientific ideas the situation becomes more challenging. For example, consider the sequence of events undertaken to introduce 'forces' to pupils during their primary years. We usually begin by exploring pushes and pulls, something the pupils experience and interact with on a day-to-day basis. Later we move on to the abstract idea of gravity, often relating it to the concept of density. Think about the progressive steps we outline in teaching density (see Figure 1.1).

This is an example of progression in terms of the *scope* of a concept to be learnt: the depth of understanding and the degree of complexity for example that the pupil is expected to take on board. The amount of guidance and support they are given and indeed require is dependent on several factors. We return to this idea of progression, scope and guidance in Chapter 4. Too often as teachers we are accused of 'spoon-feeding' our pupils, but there are several reasons for doing this:

- It could be that we consider it the only way to ensure that our pupils receive the information they need for assessment purposes (the product view of education),
  - and for that reason we are often afraid to surrender control of their learning to the pupils.
- It could be that the pupils themselves demand to know the answers ('don't teach me, just tell me what I need to know!')
  - *I have often experienced this with older students.*
- It could be that owing to time constraints we have a great deal to get through in such a limited amount of time that '... quite frankly there's no time for this "woolly" approach to education. So just give the pupils the information and move on!'

Figure 1.1 Progression within the concept: density

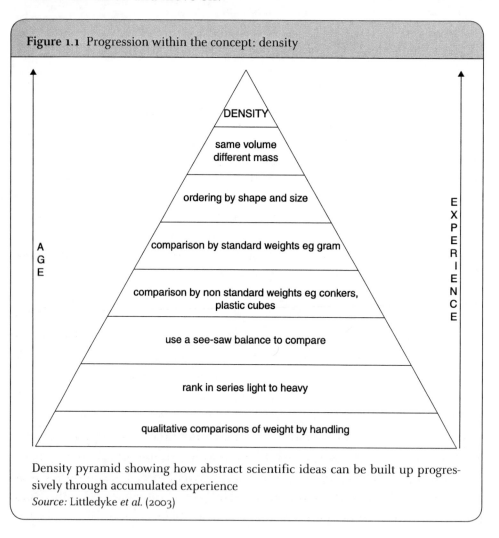

Density pyramid showing how abstract scientific ideas can be built up progressively through accumulated experience
Source: Littledyke *et al.* (2003)

These are reasons that evoke a variety of responses, but consider how much the pupils are really taking away with them in terms of learning and value added from each of these scenarios. Unless pupils go beyond gaining the required information, to actually being able to do something meaningful with it, they will not progress. Their learning will be shallow and superficial without any depth of understanding or retention. So in our teaching, differentiation in terms of scope and guidance is fundamental to the learning process and the development of independent learners. It forms the cornerstone of effective progression and ultimately, successful transition. We revisit this in greater depth over the next few chapters.

So why is it important to develop our pupils as independent learners?

If the above paragraph is true, giving increasing responsibility for learning to the pupil together with the subsequent challenges that accompany this is time-consuming, challenging and potentially risky in attainment terms. Why then are we encouraged to develop pupils who are independent learners? Have a go at the next Activity (1.9):

Activity 1.9 Potential benefits of being an independent learner

- What, from a pupil's perspective, do you consider to be the benefits of being an independent learner (within the definition stated above)?
- What benefits will it bestow on you as a teacher?
- What do you consider are the potential disadvantages of becoming an independent learner?

Once again, share your answers with a colleague.

Over the years there has been considerable educational research conducted into how pupils learn in science education and the implications of an essentially didactic, assessment-led curriculum, whereby pupils may be active physically but are not necessarily active and engaged cognitively. Developing the skills and competences of independent learning has frequently been presented as a solution to this ever prevalent situation (Millar, 1989; Osborne and Dillon, 2008; Lakin, 2010). Some of the reasons put forward include:

- Placing increasing responsibility for learning on the learner themselves acts as a motivational driver for learning: the pupil is more likely to want to learn if they are directly involved in the nature, content and design of the learning process. There are of course limitations to this, take for example the opening quote for this chapter, what if the man doesn't *want* to fish or doesn't *like* fish? These are but additional barriers to the process but not insurmountable; there are ways around them as we will see in Chapters 3, 4, 5 and especially Chapter 6.

- The learner becomes increasingly in control of their decisions and hence their learning. This can be an enormous benefit because with help and guidance they can set a pace and level of development that is right for them. This is a challenging idea that requires cognitive engagement if it is to be successful (not just a case of taking the easiest option); as we see in Chapter 3, it is something that pupils are already encouraged do to varying degrees.

- The impact in terms of learning is the greatest benefit: research evidence suggests that pupils will develop understanding and with appropriate help and guidance will create meaning and retain what they have learnt (Lakin, 2004; Osborne and Dillon, 2008; Ross *et al.*, 2010). The following analogy in Activity 1.10 explains this perspective:

Activity 1.10 Cycling analogy

(Image by G. Burch, 2012)

Compare that last bullet point with the analogy of a child learning to ride a bike. By distilling the process the following steps emerge:

- Begin with the use of stabilizers and a helping hand
- Then being able to ride with just one stabilizer and then none at all

- The first rather wobbly ride on your own and then improving with practice
- Developing 'road sense' and special awareness through practice and experience
- Being able to ride a bike again several years later after not having ridden one for a length of time.

How does this compare with the type of learning we have been exploring? Once again discuss this with a colleague or friend. Some comments on this are included at the end of this chapter.

- Finally, one of the most significant potential benefits of independent learning is that there is invariably some element of self-satisfaction with it. With the learner being in the driving seat there is a greater chance that the activity whatever it may be will interest, motivate and hopefully inspire, whilst bringing about some element of pleasure as well!

Unpicking

Take a few minutes to look back over the activities featured in this chapter; think about the approach taken with each. First you were asked to carry out a specific task but in nearly every case you were invited to externalize your answer by either writing it down or verbalizing it to someone else. By doing so you were rehearsing and confirming your thoughts. The ideal scenario is to discuss them: first articulating your thoughts in such a way that the other person can understand them, then you need to listen to their view on the situation (it helps if they have some experience of the topic). It may not always be possible to discuss your thoughts, but externalizing visually still has its benefits. Representing your thoughts as a concept map or flow diagram requires you to use the higher-level skills of analysis and synthesis. These opportunities when presented to pupils can be immensely beneficial and go some way to developing those skills of independent thought and learning we are seeking to augment. This is an example of 'reformulation': a process by which the learner revisits and restates their interpretation of the information in question. It is an invaluable aspect of the learning process and one to be encouraged. Think carefully about the form you wish this process to take; it may not be appropriate to use words as this could distract from the emphasis of the task because, for example, the pupil may have difficulty with writing or with the use of English. Perhaps suggest a variety of alternative vehicles such as drawings, photographs and sound recordings as a means of capturing and communicating ideas.

Summary

During this chapter we developed a definition for 'independent learning', one which began by exploring ownership and taking responsibility for one's learning but went on to emphasize the importance of autonomy, creativity and critical thinking. To achieve this level of independence requires differentiation in terms of both the scope of the learning and the amount and type of guidance afforded by the teacher. The focus was directed towards the learner being central to the learning process and the content being relevant, useful and retained; hence the quote heading the chapter.

The benefits of becoming an independent learner were explored initially in terms of motivation and personal drive, then later with regard to long-term impact and knowledge retention as the learner begins to create meaning and develop understanding. The idea of reformulation: externalizing, applying and synthesizing newly acquired knowledge and understanding was introduced through the various activities supporting this chapter. This important and fundamental aspect of learning takes the process further and to be fully effective demands interaction and exchange with others. Interdependent learning features significantly in the second half of the book but before then in Chapter 2 we delve deeper into our perception of knowledge, science and education. We go on to analyse the many factors influencing our teaching and the pupils' learning.

Table 1.3 Progression in teaching and learning

Teacher dependent	→	Teacher independent
Simple	→	Complex
Describe	→	Explain
Use everyday language	→	Using scientific language
Concrete level of operation	→	Abstract level of operation
Copy word for word	→	Summarize and abridge

Cycling analogy

This analogy illustrates admirably the development of a skill that once established can generally be picked up again many years later providing the cyclist is physically able and has a bike. You may wobble a bit at first but it will not take long for the skill to resurface. So how similar is this to independent learning? There are several similarities:

- Riding a bike is a skill that will improve and can be perfected with practice.

- Although 'cycling' generally involves just you and the bike, *riding*, like the outcome of being an independent learner, can involve and influence others as well as yourself. It is here that the analogy begins to break down: cycling with others may enhance the pleasure of riding and possibly perfect the skill, but it is not a necessary requirement of developing the skill of being able to ride. With *independent learning* on the other hand, interaction and cognitive exchange with others is a fundamental aspect of developing the skills associated with cognitive autonomy and personal reflectiveness; a perspective we explore in the later chapters of this book.

2 Classroom application

'...it's a philosophy'...

(The Lion King)

Introduction

In Chapter 1 we focused on learning and the learning process particularly with regard to progression and transition. Emphasis was given to the importance and relevance of developing independent learners; those who are autonomous and creative in their thinking and constructively critical of their understanding. This chapter introduces a philosophical tenor to the learning process. It begins by inviting you to consider how you view science and whether it differs from your view of science education. We move on to consider why this insight is important, exploring its relationship with established theories of learning and the pedagogy that surrounds them. The focus then turns to the many factors affecting and influencing learning. There is recognition of two key driving forces at play in any learning process, namely 'motivation' and 'confidence', both of which are explored and their impact discussed. From these discussions, opportunities for progression in learning are drawn out. Particular emphasis will be given to progression from being a dependent learner to becoming an independent learner.

The chapter concludes by identifying the skills, processes and competences fundamental to the development and enhancement of independent learning in science education, using examples from the primary and transitional education settings.

As you progress through the chapter once again reflect upon how you and your pupils learn and consider why you do things in the way you do:

how much do you think this has to do with the way you view science and science education?

> **Key ideas in this chapter:** Motivation (both intrinsic and extrinsic) and confidence in relation to developing independent learning; skills, processes and competences applicable to a range of learners; the role of learning theory in primary education; the importance of a positive learning environment, wherever that may be.

Some definitions ...

One of the most influencing factors in terms of your own learning and teaching is your perception of education, in particular science education, and how this relates to and compares with your perception of science generally.

Try answering the question in Activity 2.1:

> ### Activity 2.1 Terminology
>
> Think about the term 'education' – what does it mean to you?
>
> Is it something that can be acquired or 'topped up', like adding to your collection of model cars, handbags or shoes, most of which will remain as trophies of bygone days? Or do you see education as something broader than this; something that needs assimilating, using and revisiting regularly? Something that becomes your own and is unique to you?
>
> Or do you see it as something altogether different? Make a record of your thoughts and the factors influential in shaping this view.

The dictionary definition for 'education' tends to be abstract and rather vague, falling short of any substantial insight into the term:

1   the process of educating or being educated;
2   the theory and practice of teaching;
3   information about or training in a particular subject;
4   an enlightening experience.

Consider again your answers to the last activity. It may be interesting to find out how your view of education compares with that of your peers and your colleagues at school. You will find several similarities but also many differences. Taking this a stage further, if you ask the question: 'What is the purpose of education?' you may discover more in-depth responses but once again the question evokes a range of answers. This is largely because we each develop our own perception of the term based on previous personal and professional experiences. These are unique to the owner and influence views, perceptions and often actions. With this in mind what, therefore, is the role of the teacher in education? Gallimore and Tharp (1990) identified six aspects of a teacher's role, changing rapidly as the varying needs arose in the classroom environment:

1 *Modelling*   Pupils will need to have some indication of the nature, format and framework associated with a set task. The teacher models these particular aspects drawing in contributions from the pupils to help clarify and direct the task.

2 *Contingency manager*   Orchestrating any activity within a classroom requires careful direction and management. Guidance and mediation on the part of the teacher are required to foster confidence and self-disciplined participation by the pupils.

3 *Giving feedback*   Pupils need the assurance and reassurance that what they are doing is appropriate and envisaged. The teacher gives formative feedback throughout the task, informing progress, and summative feedback, informing development.

4 *Instructor*   Hennessey, in Littledyke and Huxford (1998), gives a delightful account of how a teacher must act as an instructor even in a learner-centred activity. Set within the context of teaching music composition she states that instruction is of fundamental importance in developing 'specialist tools of thinking and making'. She goes on to explain that composing techniques and the musical understanding expressed in a composition arise through some form of instruction whether 'directly (taught) or indirectly (caught)' (p. 171).

5 *Posing questions*   Throughout our lessons, as teachers we employ a variety of questioning techniques for an assortment of reasons, the main reason being to assess performance and attainment. As we see later in Chapter 4, questioning to assist learning aims to produce mental questions that the pupil may not or cannot produce alone.

6 *Structuring cognitive development* Fundamental to the development of pupils as independent learners, I see this role of organizing and giving structure to pupils' thoughts and actions as being pivotal. It draws on the pupils' previous learning enabling them, with guidance, to make connections and intentions explicit thereby ensuring future actions have meaning and context.

Consider your own experiences in the classroom; how many of these roles do you recognize? Indeed, are there others not subsumed within the categories mentioned above?

So far the focus has been on education per se, but what about science education? Some educational theorists (Millar, 1989; Osborne and Dillon, 2008) suggest that teaching science in the school curriculum is unique in its demands and challenges. They would state that, being science educationalists, but the reasons go deeper than a bias towards their own subject specialism. Their argument incorporates more philosophical overtones. To understand this we must first examine our own view of science and science education.

Consider Table 2.1 in relation to your understanding of science and decide where you stand along this spectrum. Your decision will be informed by your own experiences but may also be framed by your cultural and any religious beliefs you hold. These factors will consciously or subconsciously influence and help formulate your response.

Table 2.1 Our perception of science	
Extremes of our understanding of science	
• Scientific exploration is theory-neutral, mainly from objective observations	• Scientific exploration is theory-laden
• The progression of science is a process of conceptual addition	• Progression of science encounters a series of conceptual changes or 'revolutions'
• Science knowledge is discovered	• Scientific knowledge is invented
• The development of science is a process of individual discovery	• The development of science relies on the social negotiations within the science community
• Science is culture-independent	• Science is culture-dependent

With the outcomes of this exercise in mind revisit Table 2.1 but this time replace the term 'science' with 'science education'. Does your position along the spectrum alter? If so how and why; if not, why not? Which additional factors have influenced your response? You may not have asked yourself the type of questions posed in the above exercise before but, as with many philosophical questions, an element of subjectivity will preside in the answers. From a professional perspective, as teachers we must recognize that our fundamental beliefs, whether covertly or overtly, help shape the way we perceive and teach science.

When we think about how science works in the world of scientific research, there are some elements akin to the approach we purport in school, for example:

- precise questions are asked and relevant variables identified and regulated;
- hypotheses are formulated based on basic observations;
- then experiments are designed and carried out to provide answers to the questions posed in the beginning;
- the evidence-based knowledge induced from these findings is then used to understand the natural world, make predictions about future events, advance technical and environmental understanding and underpin industrial output.

What we do not necessarily recognize is that most research carried out today is far from value-free. Funding has to be sought and this comes from industry and the government. To gain funding for scientific research is a highly competitive and value-laden process; funded areas tend to be within one of the 'hotspot' fields of research such as cancer and bio-molecular studies.

The focus on scientific research described above forms only one aspect of the science education curriculum we teach in schools. Likewise only a very small percentage of our pupils will aspire to this aspect of science in their future lives. What of the majority of pupils who do not follow this career pathway? Their understanding of science, the 'knowledge' it sustains and the impact it ensues, is a very different 'need'. How can we support and engage them?

To answer this question we must return to our view of science and with it our perception of 'knowledge'. Within philosophy two key world views of knowledge are recognized:

- *positivism*, akin to the view of a research scientist described above, claiming that the world we perceive is '. . . straightforwardly the one that is out there' (Thomas, 2009: 75);

- counter to this view is *interpretivism*, claiming that the world is not straightforwardly perceived because it is constructed by each of us in a different way.

To illustrate this, consider Case Study 2.1.

Case Study 2.1 In search of Aira Force or how not to climb Helvellyn

A case study (1)

The postcard guides 'easy walks' suggested an interesting walk starting and finishing at a car park and taking in the magnificent Aira Force waterfall in the Lake District. It would take an hour and landmarks were identified to mark the way. What could be easier?

The problem was one car park looks very much like another along the stretch of road in question, even down to the river running along the left-hand side and the information building (which was closed at the time of commencing the walk). So we set off deciding that we were in the correct place, and convincing ourselves that the wooden bridge over the river could with some stretch of the imagination be described as a stile.

Not having explored this area before we innocently walked on, enjoying the view, not too worried that the stated 'spectacular views of the lake' were, in reality masked by a row of tall full-foliaged trees – well it was summer! An hour passed with no waterfall in sight. We walked on, just over the next rise and around the next hill, making a few excuses for the mismatch of identified landmarks en route. The path stretched for miles in front of us and it climbed! Again no waterfall in sight.

A fellow traveller came striding by and we engaged in conversation, mentioning Aira Force and our seeming inadequacies in 'postcard' map-reading. To our dismay we discovered that the car park for the much sought after waterfall was a mile or so further along the main road; you really couldn't miss it! To make matters worse we were now two hours along the upward track to Helvellyn, one of the highest fells in the Lake District and not best prepared!

Source: After Lakin (2012)

Two key points emerged from that case study. First, we 'see' what we want to see and with very little effort can actually convince ourselves that what we observe is what we are expecting or expected to see. I have come across this on several occasions with pupils examining specimens under the microscope; they see what they believe they should be seeing and it is not until they have externalized their interpretations either through drawings or dialogue that it becomes clear that what the student is interpreting as the desired object was indeed, for example, an air bubble!

Second, the other key point arising from the case study was the important role other people played in the event. The fellow traveller, having significant local knowledge about the area, was immediately able to identify our problem and put us back on the right track. Our perception of the surroundings and the decisions we made, based on naive interpretation, put us in the wrong place with its associated implications. In teaching we recognize the importance of interpretivism and give credence to the learner's construction of knowledge; valuing all ideas and views arising from exploration and investigation. However, we must recognize their limitations and, in science especially, have a set of accepted facts that need to be mastered and taken on board by the learner. The challenge for the teacher is to change the learner's view or 'misconception'.

Pause for a moment and consider the essence of that last sentence: two opposing views of knowledge are suggested, the accepted knowledge of science that we teach through the curriculum and the naïve (Ross *et al.*, 2010) or alternative knowledge learners bring with them to the classroom under the guise of 'misconceptions'. During our teaching of science we aim to change pupils' own ideas into ones more consistent with scientific views. Our approach to this often involves activities enabling our pupils to express or externalize their ideas. What happens next is less uniform; sometimes we present the pupils with a discrepant event, conflicting with their view, or we use the pupils' view as the basis for a prediction and test its validity. These two approaches to instruction seemingly associate with two philosophical views of knowledge, the extremes of which are summarized in Table 2.2.

Now compare these extremes with the spectrum of views of science outlined in Table 2.1 earlier. The similarities are obvious, because essentially they describe the same thing – 'knowledge' – whether we express it in scientific terms or in our own 'everyday' terms. There is, however, a very significant difference and that is the emphasis on 'evidence'. Knowledge derived through the scientific process is evidence-based. That derived

Table 2.2 Two major philosophical views of knowledge	
Positivism	Interpretivism
• Information is studied objectively	• Knowledge is everywhere
• Knowledge is out there to be found or discovered	• Knowledge is socially constructed
• General explanations inform the specific	• All kinds of information are valid and worthy to be called 'knowledge'
• The process undertaken is value-free, therefore, all efforts are employed to reduce researcher bias	• Specific situations can be used to inform each other • The process is recognizably value-laden

through an interpretivistic approach is arguably 'evidence-based' but seldom is it scientific evidence: if it was it would be described as such. From a teaching perspective, we must remember that we cannot teach a body of knowledge by 'transmission'; the learner will always interpret and construct that knowledge personally. It is from this fundamental source that misunderstanding and misconceptions emanate. We all do this and these 'alternative ideas' can be difficult to challenge and sometimes filter through in our teaching.

The way we teach

Research evidence (Lakin, 2010; Osborne and Dillon, 2008; Driver and Bell, 1986) suggests that there is often a mismatch between our perception of the subject we teach and the way we teach it. The positivistic view of science, reinforced by a curriculum quite rightly emphasizing the nature and processes of sciences, lies counter to our often held view of knowledge and understanding of the learning process. That is until we consider our objective-led assessment procedures that strengthen the positivistic view of science while failing to test the interpretivistic approaches used in our teaching. However, I digress, we return to assessment with its benefits and limitations in Chapter 3. So what about the *way* we teach; what apart from our personal philosophy influences and determines how we carry out our various roles in the classroom?

Much has been written from educational research about the way children learn and the resulting theories and suggested approaches significantly impact on the way we teach, as we aim to maximize the learning process. Educational theory underpins much of the initial and professional development programmes in all curriculum subjects, but especially science. Activity 2.2 highlights some of the major theories and ideas arising from educational research over the years. See if you can match the names with their definitions.

Activity 2.2 Learning theories

Below are some recognized theories and approaches to teaching and learning. Their definitions have been mixed up; match the theory or approach to its appropriate definition.

Theories and approaches Definition

Co-constructed learning (1) In the form popularized (though not invented) by Alistair Smith, this approach draws heavily on brain-based learning. Building on neuro-linguistic programming it offers strategies that would enable students to learn more naturally, more effectively and faster. Smith's approach advocates a four-stage learning cycle: connect, activate, demonstrate, consolidate.

Accelerated learning (2) Systematic development of the skills, dispositions and knowledge needed to become an effective, independent learner. An important component of this approach is pupils reflecting on, learning about and learning for the 'learning process' itself.

Differentiated learning	(3) A new term for an old idea. Learning is most effective when it is designed jointly by the teacher and pupils through a process of negotiation.
Constructivism	(4) Based on the work of Black and Wiliam from King's College London, this approach featured in the national strategies. It is underpinned by the belief that the learner constructs meaning and develops understanding by drawing on previous and present experiences. Their research demonstrated that giving students regular, diagnostic, precise, actionable, written or verbal feedback is probably the most powerful way to improve performance.
Learning to learn and meta-learning	(5) A current government drive, which has become a buzz-word, officially defined as 'tailoring education to individual needs, interests and aptitudes so as to ensure that every pupil achieves and reaches the highest standards possible' (DCFS, 2007).
Thinking skills and metacognition	(6) A relatively old philosophical position that learning cannot be transferred. It can only be constructed in the mind of each learner, who must make their own meaning based on what they bring to the learning experience (in terms of prior knowledge, understanding, misunderstanding, baggage and so on). This fundamental notion has been confirmed by the findings of neuroscience and has been given new life: learning is a mentally active process.

Assessment for learning	(7)	Deliberate development of students' thinking capacities. Various models and programmes exist, such as CASE and Philosophy for Children. The McGuinness Report (1999) effectively determined five cross-phase and cross-curricular categories associated with this, together with the process of reflecting on and gaining control over one's own thinking behaviours.
Personalized learning	(8)	The long-standing idea that learning activities, resources and support should be matched as precisely as possible to learners' individual needs, be they 'gifted and talented' or 'challenged' in some way. The intention is that every single student should receive the most appropriate curriculum and learning experience.

After Lakin (2012)

The answers are provided in Table 2.3 at the end of this chapter. Can you recognize any of these theories or approaches being adopted or influential in your own school or classroom?

What Activity 2.2 tells us is that not only are there several theories and approaches to learning and teaching but also that there is no one definitive way we learn or how we should teach.

Nonetheless, for nearly three decades pedagogic constructivism has assumed the heady status of a 'super theory', arguably underpinning the way science education is taught in schools. This approach to teaching and learning encourages the use of 'active learning' techniques and relies on expert 'scaffolding' by the teacher (Driver *et al.*, 1994; Ross *et al.*, 2010). The former are defined as activities and techniques that encourage the learner to '... assess evidence, negotiate, make decisions, solve problems, work independently and in groups, and learn from each other' (Ross *et al.*, 2010: 25). The use of the metaphor 'scaffolding' to describe the teacher's role in developing new concepts aligns with providing opportunities through activities, problems and models to stimulate interaction and develop appropriate experiences. We use language and other stimuli to assist our pupils in constructing solutions to problems posed. The long-term aim, however, is to enable them to do this unaided. The degree of support should vary according to the needs of the learner. Examples of strategies and activities to promote 'active learning' and other approaches to teaching and learning mentioned in Table 2.3 are discussed in Chapter 3.

The constructivist approach, although modified by various educationalists, adheres to a generally agreed format as summarized in Box 2.1.

Box 2.1 Constructivist approach to teaching and learning

This approach to teaching and learning begins by eliciting the learner's current understanding of the phenomenon in question. For example, consider the way light is refracted when it passes through different media: adopting a constructivist approach the teacher first elicits the pupils' ideas by asking them why they think the sky is blue. A variety of answers may be received ranging from the sky reflecting the sea, to sunlight being scattered or refracted as it travels through the Earth's atmosphere.

Depending on the type of answer received the teacher will present a series of activities or experiments for the pupils to undertake as a means of either challenging or developing the pupils' understanding depending on how closely their ideas aligned with the established scientific view of this phenomenon. This is referred to as intervention and involves varying degrees of teacher 'scaffolding'. The individual pupil must then take ownership of the explanation to ensure 'deep' rather than 'surface' understanding takes place. To achieve this, the teacher encourages the pupil to test out their understanding by applying it to other situations and explaining it to their peers. This 'reformulation' process enables the pupil to tease out those areas of cognitive/mental conflict that may exist preventing them from fully understanding the phenomenon.

There is considerable evidence from educational research that pupils construct their own understanding about scientific phenomena in the world around them even before they are exposed to formal teaching (for example see Driver *et al.*, 1994; Osborne and Dillion, 2008). These personal ideas make sense to pupils because they are based on their everyday experiences. As mentioned previously, it is these alternative ideas or misconceptions that as teachers we aim to challenge if they do not match the accepted scientific one. When contemplating this situation it becomes apparent that we are dealing with both views of knowledge as identified in Table 2.2. The pupils' perception of the world around them and the knowledge they construct from that is akin to the interpretivistic view of knowledge. Indeed, philosophical constructivism is a form of interpretivism. The scientific knowledge and information that we as teachers aim to impart to our pupils is presented through a positivistic perspective of science. The problem arises when we try to align our approach to teaching science purely within a pedagogic constructivist framework; the danger of this was epitomized in a quote by Osborne almost 10 years ago:

> the advocates of constructivists methods of teaching have failed to recognise that there is a role for telling, showing and demonstrating. Teachers we are told, should 'negotiate,' 'facilitate,' 'coconstruct,' 'mediate,' 'socialise,' 'provide experiences', 'introduce,' and 'make the cultural tools of science available,' but never ever will they *tell*.
>
> (Osborne, 1996: p. 67)

There is a failure to recognize that when we learn something, we do exactly that – 'we' learn it. It is something that takes place in *our* head alone and although it can be influenced by external factors our interpretation of the information is unique to us. Now fortunately that cannot be the full story otherwise we would not be able to communicate and you would not be able to read this book, but nonetheless your interpretation of the words and the meaning I am trying to portray remains unique to you, the reader. This is why it is so important to externalize our ideas and interpretations, so that we can appreciate the similarities and differences in the way we interpret information. That being said, we cannot expect pupils to construct all the ideas, facts and theories that we call 'science' in the percentage of curriculum time we have to teach it and indeed within the limitations of equipment and other resources available in the classroom. There has to be a place for other modes of teaching, including didactic instruction and systematic learning. The expertise and professionalism of the teacher come to the fore in their selection and employment of these alternative teaching approaches as and when appropriate. Evidence from research into the use of alternative styles and approaches of teacher intervention – for example, the much acclaimed Cognitive Acceleration in Science Education (CASE) programme – suggests that the application of activities designed to develop formal operational thinking can impact positively on long-term attainment. Specific behavioural learning characteristics emerged from the research and have collectively been described as 'learning habits'. These qualities are strikingly similar to those recognized in independent learners:

- *Resilience* – the development of coping strategies to manage failure, while at the same time recognize and correct, with guidance, mistakes in their own work. Essentially there is no failure, only feedback.
- *Responsibility* – appreciating that every action has a consequence; pupils are ultimately responsible for what they do and will readily partake in peer support.
- *Resourcefulness* – being active, rather than passive in their learning.
- *Reasoning* – manifest mainly through their ability to problem-solve.
- *Reflectivity* – the ability to reflect on what they learn, what they would do differently to assist and why! This develops through promoting a sense of progression and achievement.

Certain aspects of the approach to learning and teaching promoted through the CASE activities, particularly the use of metacognition (essentially thinking about thinking) whereby thinking strategies are linked to problems in different contexts, find support from other studies of effective teaching. There is no suggestion that CASE-type work should replace the teaching of content in science; rather, it gives greater credence to a balanced teaching approach that includes a variety of styles and strategies, with pedagogic constructivism playing a significant part. We explore this in a more practical way in the following chapters.

Influencing factors affecting learning

I began this chapter by challenging you to explore your own perception of science and science education as a means of analysing the influence this perception may have on the way you view learning and, indirectly, the way you teach. Extending this further we have delved into the influence educational research can have on the approaches and strategies we use in the classroom, again impacting on the learning process. This is not to suggest that there is anything wrong with these factors; in fact, we have a great deal to thank educational research for, but it is important for reasons expressed earlier that we are aware of both these factors and take into account their influence on ourselves and the pupils we interact with. There are of course other factors that influence and shape the way we are and impact on the role we undertake in the classroom. It is to these that we now turn. Consider the factors identified in Activity 2.3 then explore and analyse their potential influence and impact on your teaching:

Activity 2.3 Factors affecting how we teach

For each of the potential influencing factors listed below give a grade on a scale of 1–5, 1 having no influence and 5 having significant influence, with regard to the level of impact you consider they have on your teaching.

- How we were taught
- A particular teacher
- Specific influences from teacher training
- Influences from other teachers: during teaching practice, in the school we teach now
- Continual Professional Development (CPD) courses/workshops we attend
- The government stipulations
- The school itself and the influence of the school culture
- The timetable
- Parents
- The pupils
- Others (include any of your own)

Now answer the following:

- What does the grading tell you about those factors influencing the way you teach?
- Were there any surprises?

- Are you comfortable with the outcomes?
- If you were able to change the level of impact of any of these factors which are they and how would you change them?
- What might be the outcome of that change?

Finally:

- Find someone you consider suitable to share this information with.

All these factors impact one way or another on what we teach and how we teach it. Some factors are more influential and have a greater impact than others. Some are within our control, while others are not. If these impact on the way we teach what impact will that have on our pupils' learning and what other influences are there that shape the learner and the learning process? We have touched on this already; in Chapter 1 you explored your own learning process and the outcomes of that activity will apply to some degree to your pupils as well. Two key factors driving learning were identified as 'motivation' and 'confidence'; whether separately or together they have a marked impact on the success of the learning process. When we consider how scientists of the past worked we uncover stories of serendipity: Newton and his apple; Fleming and penicillin. The story of Darwin and others; for example, Watson and Crick, Rosalyn Franklin and Maurice Wilkins, recognize a commitment to a lifetime of research and analysis driven by the 'need to know'! There are people like that today; think of David Attenborough and Dick Feynman, for example, who are both driven by philology; that love of learning and 'finding out' that is unfortunately so often a luxury in the classroom.

What has happened to the *love of learning*? How much does our education system and the way we teach stifle the natural desire to 'know' something? Our pupils do want to learn but their thirst for knowledge is driven by a different set of drivers. We live in a consumer-led society, one where consumer goods dominate and the acquisition of the latest commodity is a strong driver. Material items, whether in the form of the latest electronic piece of equipment or other artefacts that luxuriate and modernize our lives, become prizes that both motivate and determinant. I have found from my own research (Lakin, 2010) that this has become increasingly the case in education: learners of today appear to be strategic in their approach to their studies. To learn for learning sake seems to be a luxury; 'learning' (invariably shallow learning) buys them a ticket to the next stage towards their ultimate goal. In the case of my student teachers it was a piece of paper authorizing them to teach and thereby earn some money. For the pupils they will be teaching the incentive to learn and perform 'well' in class comes from a variety of sources. Within the classroom there is increasing emphasis on providing consumable rewards for the pupils in the form of sweets and other edible treats. This can be a slippery slope for the pupil but especially for the teacher who must run up a small fortune on 'prize expenses'! Then there are the parents; it appears that the rewards bestowed upon pupils to do well in tests, behave themselves accordingly, even to the extent of ensuring they eat all the food in their lunch box, has developed into a small industry of its own. While undertaking some small-scale research into the eating habits of primary school pupils I was amazed to hear how some 10- and 11-year-olds regularly traded the contents of their lunch box to ensure they all went home with an empty one, thereby ensuring they gain credit towards whatever reward they had been promised by their well-meaning and unsuspecting parents. An interesting situation but nonetheless insightful of the way our youngsters operate. It is this strategic and entrepreneurial approach to learning that as teachers we need to capitalize on in a sustainable and peda-gogic fashion.

Incentive-based reward systems and target setting have long existed within the primary and secondary classroom, ranging from the 'smiley' face at the end of a commendable piece of work to the end-of-year trophy for good attainment. This goes part way to stimulating and motivating a pupil to learn. What I am suggesting is that we capitalize on that inner drive that stirs and steers us when we really want something. Achieving our goal and attaining the reward is one thing but there is a journey of discovery and wonderment that is to be experienced on the way. Too often these experiences and the skills we can develop en route are suppressed by the desire to attain the goal whatever it may be, which once achieved shortly assumes its place in the cupboard; on the shelf or discarded along with the other trophies gained in a similar way. No one is to blame for this situation. As teachers we are subject to time and attainment pressures; as parents we want the best for our children and responding to peer and consumer pressure sometimes seems the best way to achieve that. However, as we shall see in the forth-coming chapters, there *are ways* of working within a 'must-have' society by capturing and developing those skills that such an incentive-driven nature demands. One such skill was identified by Vygotsky when he formulated his 'zones of proximal development'. He recognized the ability of the learner to self-correct or 'regulate' their own learning. This is an important capability on the part of the learner because using this skill effectively distinguishes the dependent from the independent learner. The ability to self-correct demands recognition of one's own errors and misconceptions and commands the ability to reflect upon and analyse the situation. Armed with this information, the skill is then to identify a way forward. Collectively, this practice echoes the five learning habits identified by the CASE research: resourcefulness, resilience, responsibility, reflective practice, and the ability to reason; qualities that characterize the independent learner. This was epitomized in Case Study 2.2 (part 2) of the saga: 'Aira Force revisited', when I revisited the waterfall I had missed during my previous excursion:

Case Study 2.2 Aira Force revisited

A case study (2)

A year later I revisited this walk to Aira Force. With the hindsight of experience and some careful preparation I arrived at the 'correct' car park and soon realized how all the signs and way-markers indicated on the 'easy walks' guide fell into place.

This emphasized the importance of reflection and revisiting practice. We cannot hope to get things 'right' the first time; there are so many variants and influences contributing to the way we first encounter something. We do, however, have the potential to analyse and question our experiences and it is this potential that as teachers we need to develop and hone in our pupils, whatever our subject specialism and whatever age group we teach.

Summary

The important role of constructivist pedagogy is to probe pupils' ideas and understanding about scientific phenomena, encouraging pupils to externalize and test them. As teachers we must provide opportunities through different teaching styles and approaches for the pupils to complete the important part of deep learning; that is self-regulated, autonomous processing and applying knowledge and understanding gained through experience, reflection and reformulation; independent of instruction and prescription yet not immune to influence. As we shall see in the forthcoming chapters, the role of social stimuli and discussion plays as important a role as these other defining characteristics of independent learning.

Theories and approaches	Definition
Table 2.3 Answers to Activity 2.2	
Co-constructed learning	(3)
Accelerated learning	(1)
Differentiated learning	(8) – This approach is linked to the current drive for personalized learning and has implications for inclusion. Find out more about the terms 'gifted and talented' and 'challenged' in the context of learners' individual needs.
Constructivism	(6)
Learning to learn and meta-learning	(2) – Meta-learning is the reflective element of this.
Thinking skills and metacognition	(7) – Find out more about CASE and P4C and how they can be incorporated in your own teaching. Metacognition is the process, but what are the five categories of thinking skills?
Assessment for learning	(4) – There are a number of associated techniques, such as clarifying and communicating learning outcomes, self and peer assessment, the use of no-hands-up policy, probing questioning by the teacher and no grading or numerical marking of the students' work.
Personalized learning	(5) – Hargreaves (2005) has proposed nine 'gate ways' to personalized learning, creating a framework that pulls together many current initiatives. Find out more about these.

CHAPTER 3

Promoting independent learning through existing strategies

Ice cream, screaming jelly babies and elephant toothpaste

Introduction

This chapter discusses several strategies developed from educational research over the years in relation to science education. Drawing on examples from 'active learning' techniques, 'assessment for learning' and 'assessing pupil progress' (an initiative now removed from the English National Curriculum but the principles behind which are still incorporated in classroom learning across the country), we explore how they can be used as vehicles to promote independent learning. The chapter goes on to suggest how, using these strategies, opportunities to develop the skills of an independent learner can be developed and enhanced.

Very much a practical chapter this includes ideas and tips on promoting independent learning, while emphasizing the importance not only of *active* engagement on the part of the learner but that they also actively *challenge* their ideas and thought processes. In order to achieve this they need to be fully cognizant of their ideas in the first place. The role of elicitation followed by effective feedback is fundamental here, both of which are readily explored. Taking all this on board could potentially present a minefield of ideas and challenges to the learner so there is a need to be absolutely clear what, as the teacher, we want to achieve from the learning experience and what we want our pupils to take away with them. To facilitate this we explore the use of learning outcomes in the lesson planning process.

The chapter concludes by asking where we go to next, thereby introducing the progressive and developmental themes underpinning the remaining chapters in the book.

Key ideas in this chapter: Assessment for learning, assessing pupil progress, and active learning; the significance of learning outcomes; the role of feedback to enhance independent learning.

Active learning

As we saw in Chapter 2, the constructivist approach to teaching and learning in science education places great emphasis on eliciting pupils' ideas about everyday phenomena. Developments in neurological sciences confirm findings from educational research that, for example, when presented with a new scientific concept pupils retain their original naïve ideas alongside the new one, rather than replacing them (Harlen, 2010). This suggests that pupils can hold conflicting ideas at the same time (Ross *et al.*, 2004), which places even greater emphasis on the need for both teacher and learner to recognize these alternative ideas. They need to be expressed in such a way that they can be discussed and appropriately challenged. There are many tried and tested ways of eliciting pupils' ideas, all of which demand some action or input from the learner. A selection of these elicitation activities are presented in the Box below:

Established elicitation activities

- Ask pupils about their ideas
- Self-completion exercises
- Card sorts
- Pupils' drawings
- Concept maps
- Concept cartoons
- Using toys and puppets
- Using scientific apparatus
- Role play exercises
- Word association games
- Listening to pupils talking

Source: Adapted from Allen (2010)

One particular favourite of mine is the use of 'concept maps'. The value of such an approach to summarize concepts and ideas has been recognized and extolled for many years. Their use, however, as a means of eliciting learners' ideas about a topic and exposing misconceptions and misunder-standing is more recent but very effective. To illustrate the power and use of the concept map, I have summarized and expounded Allen's (2010) list of suggested elicitation activities in Figure 3.1. It is worth noting that in Allen's explanation of a concept map the connecting ideas are linked with a line. Ross *et al.* (2010) explain that the real power of the concept map comes from *labelling the links* (which are directional arrows) with verbs, as illustrated in the Figure 3.1. This latter approach ensures that the learner thinks about the ideas, the words used to represent them and the type and direction of the relationship between them.

Ross *et al.* explain that pupils need to be taught concept mapping in simple stages. Begin by asking them to write a word to link two other ideas or concepts. Once this basic scheme of linking ideas is established addi-tional concepts can be added to produce a complete map. The whole process and the end product can be an extremely effective learning tool.

Concept maps, as powerful as they may be, are not without their limita-tions, as is evident from Figure 3.1 where the map can become rather clut-tered. Depending on the type of vocabulary used the essence of the link could be lost: for example, under the 'indirect methods' of eliciting miscon-ceptions, the term 'Hungry Caterpillar' needs further explanation. Within the context of the map, the 'hungry caterpillar' referred unsurprisingly to the children's story-book of the same name (Carle, 1974). Allen cites this as an eminent tool for orienting thinking towards life cycles that could later be portrayed in picture form allowing the teacher to elicit relevant miscon-ceptions. Life cycles apart, recognizing that the story's main focus is the eating habits of a caterpillar, the story could indeed be used as stimulus material for healthy eating, drawing out misconceptions regarding diet, life style and obesity. This expounded potential is not evident from the concept map alone. It is important, therefore, that when pupils are engaged in producing concept maps they are encouraged to explain and discuss their thoughts with others, especially their peers.

Challenging ideas

Having elicited pupils' ideas it is important to recognize that what the pupil is implying, has stated, or clearly believes, may be a misconception. It is up

Figure 3.1 Concept map summarizing elicitation activities

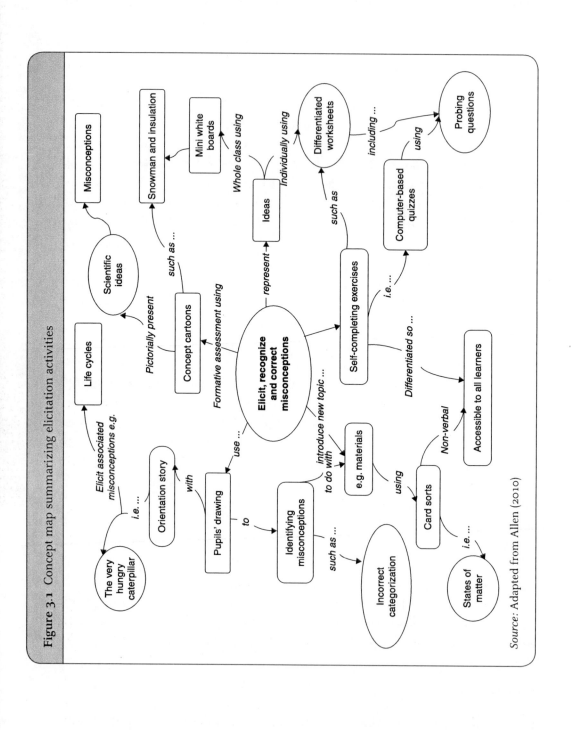

Source: Adapted from Allen (2010)

to the teacher and other professionals to identify and respond to these misconceptions. Equally there is the danger of reinforcing these alternative ideas if they are not picked up or recognized. This is where critical thinking and analysis on the part of the pupil, their peers and the teacher play a significant role, exploring and questioning the ideas as they are presented.

Assuming that any misconceptions *have* been recognized, the next step is to provide opportunities to challenge these ideas. If on the other hand elicitation responses are in tune with accepted scientific understanding, these ideas should be developed and progressed further. Whatever the outcomes of the elicitation exercise, for learning to be meaningful the learner must *engage*. This is where active learning techniques play their part. On a cautionary note, we must be careful not to equate active learning with 'child-centred' or 'discovery' learning. Both require the pupil to do something; to be actively involved. However, there is a wealth of difference between being *physically* active and being *cognitively* active. As Ross *et al.* (2010) suggest a major limitation in the use of active learning techniques is that they fall short of giving autonomy of practice to the learner. They claim that many such tasks are directional and specific; having been planned, presented and ordered by the teacher thereby removing real cognitive challenge from the exercise. The point the authors are making is that for these tasks to be effective they must ensure that the pupils *think*. A typical example of an active learning exercise is illustrated in Box 3.1. The pupils are requested to fill in the blanks in the section of text; however, it is possible to complete this exercise by a process of elimination rather than any significant cognitive engagement. To make the exercise more demanding a range of alternative words could be presented, with pupils selecting only those they consider appropriate.

Box 3.1 Cloze procedures

Techniques such as cloze procedures are designed to give pupils the opportunity to interact with the text they are reading.

In cloze procedures, gaps are left in the text and the pupils have to suggest the missing words.

Fill in the missing words in the following text:
Electricity is a way of transferring _____. It is produced from _____ and _____. Most power stations are fuelled by burning fossil fuels such as ____ or oil or gas (produced from the remains of _____).

Missing words: power stations   coal   energy
batteries   living organisms

The activity can be differentiated by including a list of the missing words; a list of words including the missing ones; no list at all or the text could be scrambled, for example, the paragraphs could be mixed up, the labelling on a diagram could be in the wrong order or, as in Activity 3.5, the task is to match the terms to their correct definitions.

Cognitive conflict

During their limited time in school it is foolhardy to expect our pupils to reinvent the whole of science (arguably the idea behind discovery learning), so their task instead has to be to try and understand the ideas scientists have used to explain the world. Ross *et al.* (2010) explain that this may involve pupils having to modify and at times reject their own ideas; referred to elsewhere as 'cognitive conflict' (Allen, 2010). Pupils often need to think about things they have never questioned before and be involved in developing ideas about phenomena they have never experienced before. To succeed at this, as suggested in Chapter 2, pupils need time to *reformulate* their ideas, thereby taking ownership and ultimately responsibility for their developmental learning. The main challenge from a pedagogic perspective is to ensure that the active learning techniques we use in our teaching present pupils with the time, opportunity and skills to enable them to do just that: to revisit, clarify and challenge their ideas and thought processes.

Opportunities to promote independent learning

The use of role play has often been espoused as a powerful means of enabling pupils to express and explore their feelings through characters other than themselves and is equally effective during intervention as in elicitation. Case study 3.1 typifies the powerful nature of role play. A class of 10- and 11-year-olds were studying food and farming as part of across-curricular citizenship theme; the role play activity in question was their end of topic activity.

Case Study 3.1

The pupils were given the task of writing and performing a short play to present at the end of term. The focus was organic versus battery-farmed egg production. Every pupil had to take part. Working in mixed ability groups to ensure help with language and literacy problems, they collectively produced their play entitled *A Dilemma*. Each group assumed the guise of particular characters:

- farmers with battery hens;
- the battery hens, themselves;
- farmers with free-range organic hens, or
- the free-range organic hens.

The main character, Mrs Hoity Toity, provided the context for the play: deciding which type of eggs to use for her Christmas cake. Each group discussed and identified the pros and cons of the debate from their character's perspective. This way they could present both sides of the argument in the play. The final production was performed to the rest of the school and respective parents. The audience was asked to help Mrs Hoity Toity to make her choice of eggs based on the information from the play. There was support for organic eggs based on taste alone, (the pupils had been given the opportunity to blind-taste organic and battery-farmed eggs) but the deciding factor was cost; parsimony won the day!

Source: After Lakin *et al.* (2004), Box 3.4, 'Assessing pupil progress'

The real educational value of this role play exercise was in providing an opportunity for the pupils to draw together and revisit the conceptual and issues-based aspects of their term's work by applying it in a new context. It gave them the opportunity to develop their skills of imagination, original and critical thought and action through enquiry, questioning, experimentation and expression: a powerful learning activity!

Another vehicle through which such opportunities are bestowed arises from one of Allen's (2010) suggested elicitation strategies: the use of educational puppets as characters towards which pupils can direct their thoughts and ideas. Puppets have long been used in primary education for such a role but the emphasis on exposing and recognizing misconceptions is more recent and exemplified in Case Study 3.2.

Case Study 3.2 'Mathilda'

At the beginning of term a Science Day was held for all pupils in a local primary school. The focus of the day was 'light and shadows' and all classes took part in a series of similar but differentiated activities relating to this topic. Six months after the event several pupils from each year group were selected at random and all took part in a discussion about the Science Day. The focus of the discussion was an educational puppet 'Mathilda'. Mathilda had completed a worksheet similar to that used during the Science Day and the various groups of pupils were asked to comment on Mathilda's worksheet. Mathilda's worksheet was carefully constructed so as to include a range of misconceptions reportedly held by pupils when developing their understanding of 'light and shadows'.

Some interesting comments arose; most pupils from early primary through to top primary had retained the fact that a 'shadow' is continuous with the object producing that shadow. Most pupils were able to distinguish between reflection and production of shadows, apart, that is, from one 9-year-old pupil and several reception or kindergarten pupils. The 9-year-old caused some concern until she later explained to Mathilda that she had missed the Science Day because she had been ill. She had, however, been at school when they learnt about reflection a term earlier.

The use of Mathilda proved to be a successful distraction from the teacher, encouraging the pupils to engage in conversation with her about the topic in hand. The teacher, not skilled in the art of ventriloquism had Mathilda whisper to her, stating that she was rather shy about speaking in public. It worked a treat – even with the older pupils!

The value of puppets as a vehicle through which pupils could express themselves has been recognized for many years; their educational value particularly in science education is more recent but reached a peak more recently. Examples include 'Ricky goes to the Antarctic' (Wood, 2010) where a primary school teacher took part in the annual Fuchs Foundation expedition to the South Pole, accompanied by a puppet called 'Ricky'. The aim was to bring some real-life scientific enquiry-based problems back to her pupils in Newham, London. During the expedition teachers and their classes were able to communicate with the Antarctic explorers and carry out problem-solving activities in the classroom relating to survival in sub-zero temperatures. The project provided a purposeful, contextual focus for the science lessons with Ricky providing stimulus and novelty.

The use of puppets is not just confined to primary education; a resource developed by a secondary school science teacher in despair of her first year pupils' lack of engagement with homework activities focuses on a dog called 'Scruff'. Enquiry and problem-solving activities have been developed in relation to this rather amiable character; needless to say a puppet depicting the animal and a range of associated activities has been developed by the Association for Science Education.

The benefit of both scenarios described above is that they capture pupils' imagination. To develop meaningful learning and deep understanding the process must go further. As emphasized earlier in this chapter, the ultimate challenge in any educational strategy is to encourage pupils to engage with the pedagogic process by being cognitively active, not merely physically active. One way of ensuring this is to encourage pupils to *think*.

Developing and enhancing 'thinking skills'

The development of 'thinking skills' and in particular the role of metacognition – 'thinking about thinking' – has transformed classroom activity since the late 1990s by presenting opportunities for high level teaching and learning. The approach to teaching and learning that empha-sizes the development of thinking skills has been advanced in association with developments in the neurological sciences. Research in this area has informed and transformed our understanding of how the brain works during the learning process. Research suggests that the development of critical thinking is fundamental to our decision-making process and, as Harlen (2010) recognizes, is significant in challenging and replacing pupils' naïve ideas about scientific concepts, thereby promoting conceptual change, once again through cognitive conflict.

To ensure permanent and not merely transitory conceptual change the learning process must be ongoing. Ideas and experiences must be revisited and changes mulled over and analysed objectively. This process of reflec-tion has become widely recognized within pedagogic circles generally and science specifically but as one would expect, becoming proficient at it is a developmental process. Levels of effectiveness depend on the degree and quality of reflection employed by the learner. A pupil between the ages of 7 and 11 can generally reflect upon their own level of knowledge and under-standing and possibly suggest in simple terms what they would need to do to progress to the next level of attainment. Likewise a pupil in the first couple of years at secondary school; but at what stage do these powers of reflection progress from the superficial 'explain something rather than describe it' to the more challenging higher-order skills that lead to concep-tual change? As exemplified earlier, to achieve conceptual change, with or without the input of an expert practioner, the learner must be actively and cognitively engaged in the learning process. Opportunities for reformula-tion should be provided to ensure ownership of ideas is achieved. Until this happens the learner's engagement is only superficial and deep learning that leads to cognitive understanding is not achieved. This demands the acquisi-tion and use of higher-order skills such as analysing, interpreting and evalu-ating information rather than simply amassing, reproducing and describing it (Hill and Woodland, 2002). Part of this process is to be able to recognize and fill the gaps in subject knowledge and understanding. This, however, begs the question '... *how can the learner know, what they don't know?*'

Analysing learning

As learners one way to identify what we do not know is to 'tease out' a concept into its various developmental components. We begin by identifying the basic principles of the concept and then undertake a series of developmental progression by identify the stages in the development of the concept. Take photosynthesis for example:

Gaps in the subject knowledge begin to appear when we ask what we need to know to progress from *understanding* that a green plant requires sunlight, 'air' and water to survive to *understanding* and indeed *explaining* that it is in fact a combination of carbon dioxide and oxygen that is needed along with the other requirements for a plant to survive. Pupils seldom make these leaps of understanding by themselves; they require expert intervention and guidance for others, usually the teacher, within their learning community. This is illustrated through Case Study 3.3, which demonstrates how scientific ideas can be portrayed and experienced using visual, auditory and kinaesthetic stimuli.

Case Study 3.3 Flower-power!

At the start of the morning session the concept of photosynthesis was introduced in outline to a class of 11-year-old pupils. A variety of strategies were used to elicit their ideas and knowledge about a plant's requirements for photosynthesis. Sunlight energy, water and carbon dioxide were all identified as components of the process, with oxygen, water and sugars being produced as end-products.

The outline of a huge sunflower was drawn in the playground and the class then acted out the various particles as they became involved and transformed during the photosynthetic process.

Later that day the pupils drew posters summarizing their learning. The activity proved extremely successful with all pupils being able to translate their earlier experiences into a comprehensive poster illustrating photosynthesis.

The approach used in Case Study 3.3 exemplifies teaching styles and strategies underpinned by neurological understandings of the way we learn encapsulated in pedagogic constructivism. The approach emphasizes that words alone are only one way of helping us formulate and reformulate ideas. The multifaceted nature of intelligence draws on all our senses and experiences and as teachers we must ensure that our teaching provides opportunities to accommodate this.

One illustration necessitates returning to the theme of 'food and farming' described earlier and the research that was undertaken at the time. As part of a national Growing Schools initiative two primary schools within the of Gloucestershire area explored the use of this cross-curricular theme in their science lessons. The use of off-site visits and activities was central to the Growing Schools project and a visit to a local farm was a focus for lessons taught in both schools. One of the products of the local farm was an organic fertilizer made from the breakdown of comfrey leaves. The production process for the fertilizer was repeated in school and provided an opportunity to investigate modern farming practices. Pupils learnt about the legislation associated with intensive farming and explored the difference between this and organic methods. They produced mind-maps summarizing the issues associated with animal welfare from the different farming practices and explored consumer choice in terms of food consumption. This culminated in an activity referred to as the 'Shopping Bag game'. Pupils were asked to make choices about the food items they were presented with and when issued with food tokens, asked to justify their purchasing decision. Drawing on information discussed in previous taught sessions and with the added influence arising from being able to taste the various products, they pondered over their various choices. In the majority of cases the pupils opted for the cheaper, highly processed product they were familiar with and could afford. The process went some way to encourage the pupils to think about why they do things and the influences that affect their decisions, as well as the conceptual aspects associated with food production.

The fundamental pedagogic message arising from the above activity is to ensure that pupils are engaged with the content of the activity sufficiently that learning takes place. Achieving this often demands aspects of creative teaching. I have attended several spectacular science events over the years, all of which have had pupils sitting on the edge of their seats, enthralled with the displays. It was these that informed this chapter's title: ice cream, screaming jelly babies and elephant toothpaste. All three were just that: *displays*. The closest the pupils got to cognitive challenge in pedagogic terms was through visual and auditory stimulus. They remember the 'oh ah' factor, but very little else. The ice cream, once it was made, was passed around to be poked and prodded by the audience. So what did they take away with them? The fact that ice cream is cold and squidgy, both of which are not new, but also perhaps that by cooling ingredients down with an 'alien substance' (liquid nitrogen) it is possible to make ice cream very quickly and easily. Nothing else, however, was explained about the process or the reason for doing it that way. So how is that any different from what happens in the classroom? In some situations, very little; the 'screaming jelly baby' is a case in point. I have observed several students and practising teachers demonstrate the 'screaming jelly baby' practical in class whereby the jelly baby, once dropped into heated potassium chlorate, bursts into flames while screaming intensely. It is a dramatic demonstration and, yes, the pupils were engaged and the message they took away with them was that science can be fun, exciting and scary. Its educational value, however, is superficial. In all cases observed there was no attempt to explain the complex chemical process involved, no explanation as to why the jelly baby responded in the way it did, no attempt to set the activity in context and relate it to everyday experiences; its educational value was of secondary importance. The teachers included it because they could and it is a spectacular demonstration. I do not disagree with this type of science in the right place and at the right time but it needs to be presented in such a way that it adds value beyond being purely entertainment.

Activity 3.2 Entertainment science

Is there a role for 'entertainment science' in the classroom?

Think about your own practice and that of your colleagues. How much of what you teach fits into this category of 'entertainment' and how can it put to good pedagogic use?

Our challenge as teachers has to be to incorporate these strategies, activities and demonstrations in such a way that they do engage, stimulate, challenge as well as entertain our pupils! No mean feat, but not insurmountable. The answer of course is already there – 'engagement' – not the 'lean-back' passive type of engagement whereby information wafts over the impartial learner. No, the 'lean-forward' active engagement that demands full cognitive participation, whereby pupils question, explore and later apply the information and experiences gained. To illustrate this we return to the 'Shopping Bag' game:

Case Study 3.4 The Shopping Bag Game

Having completed their purchasing the pupils talked knowledgeably and convincingly about why they purchased what they did, what influenced their decisions and why.

The teacher wanted to apply these developing skills of decision and justification to the wider debate of global environmental sustainability. To achieve this required more detailed information of a global scale but, more significantly, honing the pupils' debating skills. The former was achieved through a series of 'fact-finding' exercises, the latter through the use of 'diamond ranking'.

The pupils working in pairs were given a set of pre-prepared statements relating to the topic in question and encouraged to arrange the statements in a diamond shape: the most agreeable statement at the top working down to the one they felt they agreed with least. This approach allowed the pupils to externalize their own ideas and to listen and discuss each others'. The debate was amicable, and the statements were arranged and rearranged until a general consensus emerged. An example is illustrated below:

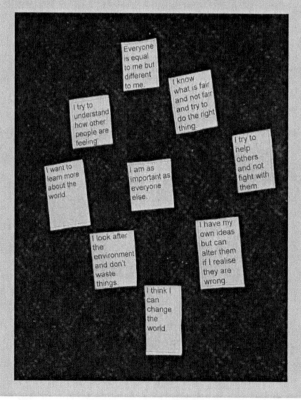

Throughout the activities and strategies described above a common theme emerging is to encourage 'externalization'; to enable pupils to express their thoughts, ideas and feelings. This is a powerful skill and from an educational perspective, a valuable source of assessment-based information. Taking full advantage of this opportunity to assess learning and progress is a skill that as teachers we must develop and fine-tune.

Assessment for learning

The term 'assessment for learning', whereby the outcomes of assessment are used to inform learning, has been present within pedagogic vocabulary for many years. It first became popular following the work of Black and Wiliam in the late 1990s. The Assessment Reform Group in 2002 aligned this type of assessment with formative practices describing it as, 'The process of seeking and interpreting evidence for use by learners and their teachers to decide where the learners are in their learning, where they need to go and how best to get there.'

Harlen (2006) summarized some of the key features arising from Black and Wiliam's work in terms of the formative use of assessment emphasizing that substantial gains in learning could be made once these features were applied:

Box 3.2 Key features of assessment for learning

- The provision of effective feedback to pupils
- The active involvement of pupils in their own learning
- Adjusting teaching to take account of the results of assessment
- A recognition of the profound influence assessment has on motivation and self-esteem of pupils, both of which are crucial influences on learning
- The need for pupils to be able to assess themselves and understand how to improve

Source: After Harlen (2006)

Before we can begin to think about the mechanisms of assessment for learning it is important to ensure that all involved (i.e. teachers, teaching assistants and most importantly pupils) know what the learning process and associated activities aim to achieve. This is where learning objectives or *intended learning outcomes* (ILOs) feature.

Activity 3.3 Identifying learning outcomes

Think about your most recent lesson and answer the following questions:

- What did you aim to achieve by it?
  - Your objectives
- What did you want your pupils to take away with them?
  - The learning outcomes
- What were you looking for as success or performance indicators?

The questions in Activity 3.3 will be easy to answer if you are in the habit of writing lesson plans, or they may require some mental searching to tease out what you had in mind. Whether formally or informally, consciously or otherwise, you will have an idea of what those objectives, outcomes and key performance indicators (KPIs) were. The terms are defined for you in Box 3.3:

Box 3.3 Some definitions of learning-related terms

Learning Objectives:

These are short-term, immediate and rapidly testable. They answer the following question: at the end of this session, what do I want my pupils to *know, do* or *understand* which will take their learning on from where it is now?

Learning Outcomes:

These describe knowledge, skills and/or understanding acquired by the learner by the end of this session that will take their learning forward.

Intended Learning Outcomes:

These are a combination of learning objectives and learning outcomes and written as a statement of intention and they will always include a *qualified* verb. Intended learning outcomes can then be assessed formatively and/or summatively (see Activity 3.4 for further definitions and explanations of these terms).

Key Performance Indicators (KPIs):

Borrowed from industry the term relates to specific criteria against which a measure can be made. Aligned directly with your objectives and learning outcomes, these criteria are used to assess success and progression towards a target for the lesson, the term and/or the year.

Source: Lakin (2010)

When planning any learning activity we often launch into the 'content', directed purely by what we want the learner to cover as a result of the lesson. This has become increasingly the case as objective setting and an assessment-driven curriculum drive the planning process in both primary and secondary classrooms. It is here that the distinction between learning objectives and learning outcomes arises. The objectives are teacher-focused and teacher-driven. The learning outcomes, however, are learner-focused and learner-driven. There has been much debate about the limitations and constraints of an objective-led curriculum; we touch on this in more detail in Chapter 4. Equally, however, a predominantly learner-driven approach runs the risk of being as limited and constraining. It is for these reasons that I present a combination of the two, aiming to reach a balance between teacher objectives or *intentions* and learner achievements and ultimately 'deep' understanding in relation to assessment outcomes.

Writing intended learning outcomes is an art in its own right and has been the subject of several development strategies and initiatives. Many teachers will be familiar with 'WALT' and 'WILF' – 'We are learning to' and 'What I'm *(the teacher)* looking for' – the first, essentially teacher objectives or intentions and the second, learning outcomes. Interestingly it is the objectives that are written collectively; that is, involving both the teacher and the learner; whereas the outcome, which should be learner-focused is actually teacher-focused, that is, what the teacher is looking for in the learner, not what the learner will be achieving. My argument here is that the focus is again on content rather than individual achievement, and the teacher is portrayed as the focus of the exercise.

The use of WALT and WILF was introduced several years ago as part of the National Strategy initiatives and are still retained in some classrooms today. An example of how they could be used is illustrated in Case Study 3.5 taken from a first year secondary lesson on energy:

Case Study 3.5 Using WALT and WILF

[*1-hour lesson on 'Energy associated with Food' with 11–12-year-old pupils*]

Some secondary schools make use of the WALT (We Are Learning To . . .) and WILF (What I am Looking For . . .) system to introduce learning objectives and outcomes.

Learning objectives: WALT can be taken directly from your medium-term planning exercise or prepared schemes of work. These outline what the pupils are going to learn during the lesson. They are usually related to aspects of knowledge and understanding and/or skills.

- Know that energy is measured in joules and kilojoules.
- Recognize that different foods release different amounts of energy when respired and that energy is needed for all animals to live.
- Explore how the energy available through respired food depends on its constituents and requires oxygen (air) as in the burning or combustion process.

- Begin to calculate the energy value available from meals.

Learning outcomes: WILF indicates what the pupils will be able to do by the end of the lesson. They can be differentiated according to the 'all must', 'some should' and 'a few could' phrases associated with several prepared schemes of work, but try differentiating further by carefully selecting the verb associated with the action. This is explored later in this chapter and illustrated below.

- All pupils will:
  - o state the unit of energy;
  - o know at 'burning food' in our bodies is called respiration and supplies energy for animals to live;
  - o be able to identify the energy available on food labels;
  - o know that air is needed to enable us to respire food.

- Most pupils will:
  - o know that 1 kJ = 1000J;
  - o recognize which foods have the highest energy available per 100 g;
  - o understand how the energy available is displayed on food labels.

- Some pupils will:
  - o understand why fat and sugar release more energy;
  - o be able to do simple calculations using energy in joules;
  - o explain where the body releases energy and uses energy (in cells).

Source: Adapted from Ross *et al.* (2010)

In contrast to WALT and WILF, an *intended learning outcome* approach encapsulates both objectives and learning outcomes, while enabling an element of progression and differentiation. It is the all important *'verb'* mentioned in Box 3.3 that qualifies the statement. Indicative levels of progression and differentiation, however, do not come from the verb alone but from the degree of *scope* and *guidance* associated with it. These terms need explanation, but as a teacher you apply them on a regular basis:

- *Scope* refers to *what* the pupils are being asked to do:
  - the detail of coverage, the depth of understanding and the amount of complexity demanded by a particular activity.
- *Guidance,* on the other hand, refers to the support and 'scaffolding' afforded by the teacher and others in the learning situation. In terms of progression and differentiation this relates to:
- How much support and direction the pupil will be given and how much they are encouraged and capable of doing *independently* (in all interpretations of the term).

An example of an intended learning outcome incorporating both scope and guidance is given as follows:

- Can work with adult help to do simple calculations using energy in joules.
- With the help of prepared worked examples, can work with a partner to do simple calculations using energy in joules.
- Can work unassisted to do simple calculations using energy in joules.

It is worth noting that the statement of guidance focuses on the support and direction the pupils will receive. Remember that this can then be differentiated according to individual needs. This is illustrated by general statements of differentiation as cited in the energy lesson example illustrated in Case Study 3.4. The nature, detail and scope of the exercise are usually linked to the verb in the intended learning outcome. Progression can be built in via appropriately selected vocabulary; Table 3.1 gives some examples.

Progression underpinning the vocabulary in Table 3.1 adheres to a hierarchical taxonomy introduced by Bloom (1965) in the mid-1950s. The idea of progression in these terms is explored in more detail in Chapter 4 where its use in intended learning outcomes is translated into a means of assessment using appropriately styled questions.

Table 3.1 Verbs for use in writing intended learning outcomes				
Draw	State	Record	Recognize	Identify
Sort	Describe	Select	Present	Locate information from text
Decide	Discuss	Define	Classify	Explain how
Devise	Calculate	Interpret	Construct	Clarify
Plan	Predict	Conclude	Solve	Determine the key points from ...
Formulate	Explain why	Use the pattern to ...	Reorganize	Explain the differences between ...
Link/make connections between ...	Use the idea of ... to ...	Uses a model of ... to ...	Provide evidence for ...	Evaluate the evidence for ...

Source: After Ross *et al.* (2004)

Alignment between carefully written intended learning outcomes and assessment has long been recommended, with emphasis being given not only to summative assessment but perhaps more significantly to formative assessment. Before exploring this alignment in more detail some terms already referred to need clarification.

Activity 3.5 Some more definitions

Several assessment-related terms have already been introduced and a selection is included below. Their definitions, however, have been mixed up.

Test your understanding of these terms by matching the definition below to its appropriate term:

Assessment of learning	Informs our reflective practice and is often synonymous with it.
Formative assessment	Evaluating teaching and learning. Possibly involves two ways of reflecting: reflection-on-action (takes place after the event) and reflection-in-action (takes place during the event and can inform development).
Summative assessment	Involves each individual in a consideration of their own work.
Assessment for learning	Carried out during the period of learning and is used to inform future practice. Usually informal.
Self-assessment	Carried out at the end of a period of learning and looks back on achievement. Essentially assessment of learning. Usually formal testing..
Peer assessment	Takes into account the 'baggage/bias' we bring with us to our teaching.
Assessment about learning	Involves students assessing the work of their peers.
Reflective practice	Carried out during the period of learning and is used to inform future practice. Synonymous with 'formative learning'.
Reflexive practice	Carried out at the end of a period of learning and looks back on achievement. Synonymous with 'summative assessment'.

You can check your answers against the table at the end of the chapter.

On a day-to-day, lesson-by-lesson basis, the link between intended learning outcomes and assessment is formative. It is important to recognize that we often assess informally without thinking: constantly seeking information about pupils' understanding and progression in relation to our objectives and their apparent needs. By formalizing this process we run the risk of marginalizing a process that we often do by instinct. Harlen (2006) recognized this resulting scenario and explained that formative assessment is not an 'add-on' to our teaching; rather, it should be integral to the learning and teaching process. We need to establish a compromise between what we do instinctively and the good practice arising from consciously aligning assessment with our intentions and the pupils' learning. Opportunities for constructive formative assessment, whether formal or informal, need to be sought and acted upon. Harlen goes on to describe a formative assessment cycle illustrating how she envisages the essential features of formative assessment put into practice.

Being a cyclical process the outcomes of decisions at particular times alter the learning activity and enable the learner to make progress towards achieving the desired goal. This will lead to further activities, during which more evidence is collected and interpreted; again leading to decisions about future progress.

Figure 3.2 The formative assessment cycle

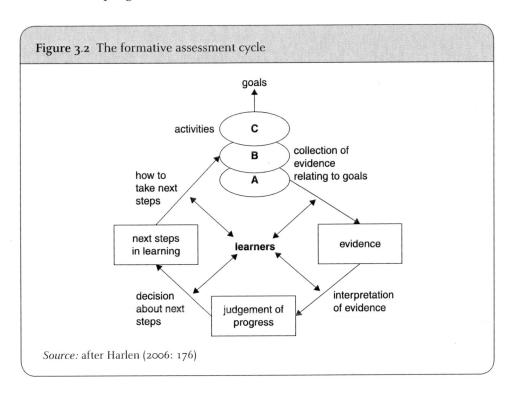

Source: after Harlen (2006: 176)

Activity 3.6 Revisiting formative assessment

This activity revisits the idea of Harlen's formative assessment cycle in the light of your own practice.

Consider the topic or scheme of work you are currently undertaking with your class. How does Harlen's cycle match with your formative assessment opportunities?

To help identify a match, answer the following questions:

- How do you set goals in relation to the activities your pupils carry out?

- What evidence is collected and how does this relate to the goals identified above?

- How and when do you judge progress against these goals?

- How do you decide the next steps to take in the learning process?

- What part do the pupils as learners play in this sequence of events?

Although Harlen mentions both the teacher and learner gathering evidence, often an approach like this is viewed predominantly from the teacher's perspective, with only a cursory mention of the role of the learner in ensuring progression takes place. Achieving learner potential in this I see as the pinnacle of independent learning, but the learner has to be *enabled* and *encouraged* in achieving this.

Assessment of pupil progress

An initiative that aptly incorporated pupil participation in the assessment process focused on ipsative assessment as well as norm-centred and criterion-referenced assessment processes. Ipsative assessment assesses the performance of the learner from their own unique perspective. The 'assessing pupil progress' initiative aimed to achieve just that and although it has now been removed from the English National Curriculum, many teachers continue to apply its philosophy.

Box 3.4 Assessing pupil progress (APP)

APP is a structured approach to in-school assessment which:

- enables teachers to make judgements about their pupils' attainment, keyed into national standards;
- develops and refines teachers' understanding of progression in their subject;
- provides diagnostic information about the strengths and weaknesses of individual pupils and groups of pupils;
- enables teachers to track pupils' progress over time;
- informs curriculum planning;
- facilitates the setting of meaningful curricular targets that can be shared with pupils and parents;
- promotes teaching that is matched to pupils' needs;
- supports the transfer of meaningful information at key transitional points, e.g. from Key Stage 2 to Key Stage 3.

A leaflet entitled 'Getting to grips with: *Assessing Pupil Progress*' is available from: www.teachernet.gov.uk/publications. Search using the ref: DCSF-00129-2009BKT-EN.

Our role as teachers and that of other learning practitioners remains crucial to the long-term development of pupil autonomy in self-assessment and target setting. Fundamental to this, however, is communication; ideally a discussion between the learner and the assessor whoever that may be. This discussion is typically referred to as 'feedback' and without it successful progress can seldom be achieved. We return to the important feature of effective feedback in Chapter 5.

Summary

In this chapter we have discussed several strategies developed from educational research in science education and have explored them in relation to independent learning. Recent neurological research points to the importance of providing pupils with opportunities to carry out the following (abridged from Harlen, 2010):

- Encourage talk, argumentation and the exchange of ideas among pupils and conversations with adults.

- Include active investigation but at the same time, promote controlled and safe behaviour.

- Involve pupils in setting goals and in assessing their achievement (essentially, the effective use of formative assessment).

- Encourage pupils to reflect on *what* they are learning and *how* they are learning (metacognition) and to establish some awareness of what they do not understand.

- Create habits of using representations and keeping notes to aid memory.

- Promote the use of scientific ideas in preference to pupils' intuitive 'naïve' ideas.

The examples discussed and explored in this chapter support all the above suggestions and are expanded and extended in the following chapters as a means of developing and enhancing pupils as independent learners.

Answers to Activity 3.5

Assessment of learning	Carried out at the end of a period of learning and looks back on achievement. Synonymous with 'summative assessment'.
Formative assessment	Carried out during the period of learning and is used to inform future practice. Usually informal.
Summative assessment	Carried out at the end of a period of learning and looks back on achievement. Essentially assessment of learning. Usually formal testing.
Assessment for learning	Carried out during the period of learning and is used to inform future practice. Synonymous with 'formative learning'.
Self-assessment	Involves each individual in a consideration of their own work.
Peer assessment	Involves students assessing the work of their peers.

Assessment about learning	Informs our reflective practice and is often synonymous with it.
Reflective practice	Evaluating teaching and learning. Possibly involves two ways of reflecting: reflection-on-action (takes place after the event) and reflection-in-action (takes place during the event and can inform development).
Reflexive practice	Takes into account the 'baggage/bias' we bring with us to our teaching.

Developing independent learning through questioning

4

'Why is an apple not a fruit, but a tomato is?'

Introduction

This pivotal chapter focuses on a fundamental learning tool and the effective use of this tool is a key skill of independent learning. It is the use of questioning. When I started to write the chapter I thought it would be relatively straightforward; after all we make use of questions in all aspects of our lives. We manipulate questioning to our own ends without even thinking about it. Children do the same and it does not take too long before they become past masters at it. Analysing this ability from an education view point and drawing out the finer details of the process has proved to be a greater task than I first envisaged.

The chapter begins by considering the role of questioning within the science classroom. As a teacher you are challenged to explore your use of questions, noting when you ask them, to whom you ask them and for what reasons. You are encouraged to consider the types of questions you ask pupils; both for your benefit and for theirs. These activities gain dimension if another person impartially records this information. As the chapter unfolds different types of questions are examined and the impact of each identified. A progression in question style, type and complexity is introduced and aligned with various aspects of the science curriculum, namely process and concept development, and the increasing degree of learner independence associated with each. Specific strategies for developing and using such progression in questioning techniques are explained with opportunities presented to tailor these to your pupils' needs and aspirations. The chapter concludes by emphasizing the importance of giving time for reflection and reformulation as a means of encouraging pupils to initiate and construct their own questions, thereby shifting ownership and stimulus to them; a characteristic that underpins independent learning and forms the focus of Chapter 5.

> **Key ideas in this chapter**: Various types and levels of questioning and how they can be used to enable independent learning in process and content-oriented learning in science; the role of reflection and reformulation for both teachers and pupils in stimulating questions and developing questioning techniques.

Why do we as teachers ask questions?

According to Kerry (2002) there are at least nine reasons for asking questions in class. These are listed below. As you read through them think critically about them: do you agree with them? Which of the reasons listed feature significantly in your own practice and which seldom occur? What if anything has been missed out?

Why do we ask questions?

- So that pupils talk – constructively and on-task
- To signal an interest in pupils, thoughts and ideas
- To stimulate interest and awaken curiosity
- To encourage a problem-solving approach to thinking
- To help pupils' externalize and verbalize what they know
- To encourage thinking aloud
- To help pupils learn from and respect one another
- To monitor the extent and deficiencies of pupil learning
- To deepen thinking and improve conceptual development

Source: Adapted from Kerry (2002)

How do we ask questions and what types do we use?

As we have seen, we use questions for a variety of reasons but have you actually analysed your own questions, the questioning techniques you use and how your pupils respond to the questions you ask them? To ensure the effective use of questions and questioning, it is important to carry out this analysis; Activity 4.1 encourages you to do just that.

Activity 4.1 Analysing your questions (I)

Select an episode of teaching that involves an extended question and answer session. Ideally video or taperecord it. If this is not possible ask a colleague to observe you. Make a record of the following:

- The number, style and type of questions you ask. These can then be categorized initially as open- (subjective response) or closed- (definitive response) style questions.

- Next consider the nature of the questions, that is, how many are factually oriented; are purely instructional; or are questions of comprehension or analysis?

- To whom are you directing the questions? Are they directed at the class generally or at specific pupils?

- Who answers the questions? Is it a random selection of pupils or the same pupils each time? How do you select who will answer? Is it only those who put up their hands or do you ask anyone?

- How much 'waiting time' do you give before seeking the answers? Do you allow the pupils to rehearse their answers by 'telling the person next to them'?

- What happens when you receive an answer you were not expecting?

This type of activity can reveal a great deal about the way we teach and indeed our perception of how pupils learn. We ask questions to gain information from our pupils, but what type of information are we trying to obtain? Unsurprisingly the majority of questions asked are factually oriented; for example:

'Who can tell me what happens to water when it is cooled to zero degrees centigrade?' or *'... the symbol we use in an electrical circuit to represent a cell?'*

We often develop this factually related style of questioning further to include questions of explanation or comprehension; for example:

'Can someone explain why the mirror in the bathroom mists up after taking a hot bath?' or *'... why the bed feels cold when you first get in it but is really warm when you come to get up in the morning?'*

Think about who answered your questions. How much control did you enforce over this? For example, consider how you selected who answered: was it solely from the pupils who put their hands up? How often did you ask questions that were targeted at specific pupils and how much time did you give them to prepare their answer? We have probably all experienced the discomfort of being singled out to answer a question 'cold' in front of a group of people. We are encouraged to put up our hand to indicate our readiness to answer the question, so the dilemma is to risk being asked if we show willing, or try to avoid answering by displaying evasive behaviour; that is, by not putting our hands up and evading eye contact, but risking being selected by the teacher. All these barriers just in response to a question! Of course, not all pupils respond in the same way and some can respond very negatively to being 'put on the spot'. However, this does not mean that we should only ask those more confident pupils who readily put up their hands. Indeed encouraging all the recipients to think silently for 30 seconds, then discuss their ideas with their neighbour, enables everyone to at least tackle the question. You are then at liberty to ask anyone what they think the answer is.

Having answered the question, what does it tell us? This depends on the type of question and how accessible it is for the respondent. Factual recall questions tell us very little about pupil learning. They mainly tell us whether or not a pupil knows the correct answer to what we are asking:

'What chemical does the symbol H represent?'

However, the answers to factual recall questions can be revealing, but this necessitates developing questioning further. It is questions of explanation and comprehension that give us some real insight into pupil learning. They must be carefully worded and initiated if they are to be effective; we return to this in more depth shortly. Before moving on, take some time to explore how your pupils respond to the questions you ask.

Activity 4.2 Analysing your questions (II)

Revisit your recording from Activity 4.1, but this time focus on the pupils and how they responded to the questions you asked.

- How many pupils were fully engaged with the question and answer session?
- How many proffered an answer/answers?
- What were the others doing?
- How many pupils asked a question of their own?
- What type of questions were these?

Pupils *do* ask questions and given sufficient thought on their part and encouragement on yours, these questions can be searching and meaningful. Often, however, they are fact seeking questions or questions of clarification and instruction. Occasionally they go deeper than that, echoing the more searching style of question mentioned earlier. These questions give real insight into the way the pupil is thinking and learning.

It is this type of question that we must nurture in our pupils, for it is these that open the doors to deeper learning, understanding and knowledge. It is questions like these, however, that as teachers we find threatening or unnerving because we cannot always answer them. Avoidance is often the plan of action! Consider for a moment how you view your role as a teacher: are you perceived as a foundation of all knowledge? We return to this in Chapter 5.

Some basic questioning skills

To enable our pupils to develop and use deeper, more probing questions, we too must develop and use this skill within our own teaching. To achieve this, we revisit the style and type of questions we use. Earlier in this chapter I mentioned questions of factual recall and of comprehension. These two levels of enquiry align with the first two levels of Bloom's Taxonomy of Educational Objectives (1965). Bloom described a hierarchical system of 'thinking' that has long been accepted within education as a developmental progression that underpins learning. As teachers we strive to develop these skills within our pupils, thereby enabling them to aspire to the higher-level skills described within Bloom's taxonomy (see Box 4.1).

Box 4.1 Bloom's taxonomy

Levels of Thinking
(Describing a progression from Level 1 to Level 6)

- Level 1 Factual or knowledge recall

- Level 2 Simple comprehension

- Level 3 Application of knowledge

- Level 4 Analysis   (Taking apart)

- Level 5 Synthesis   (Putting together)

- Level 6 Evaluation   (Judging the outcome)

The final three levels are considered 'higher-order' thinking skills, and are readily representative of the deeper levels of learning and questioning. To these I add:

- Level 7 Reflection (Reviewing personal performance or achievements)

Much has been written about Bloom's taxonomy and its application in learning and teaching. Perhaps a most useful source from a questioning point of view is the following progression chart of trigger words for use at various developmental levels within Bloom's hierarchy. The words not only define and illustrate the levels but can be used to formulate questions from the various taxa (see Table 4.1).

Table 4.1 Bloom's taxonomy 'trigger words'

Level 1 Recall	Level 2 Comprehension	Level 3 Application	Level 4 Analysis	Level 5 Synthesis	Level 6 Evaluation	Level 7 Reflection
Define	Predict	Apply	Separate	Combine	Decide	Think about
List	Associate	Demonstrate	Order	Integrate	Grade	Review
Label	Estimate	Complete	Explain	Rearrange	Test	Consider
Name	Differentiate	Illustrate	Connect	Substitute	Measure	Contemplate
Identify	Extend	Show	Divide	Plan	Recommend	Thought
Repeat	Summarize	Examine	Compare	Create	Judge	Judge
Who	Describe	Modify	Select	Invent	Compare	Assess
What	Interpret	Relate	Infer	Prepare	Assess	Critique
When	Discuss	Change	Arrange	Generalize	Critique	Cogitate about/on
Where	Extend	Classify	Analyse	Compose	Review	Muse over
Tell	Contrast	Experiment	Categorize	Modify	Justify	Deliberate
Describe	Distinguish	Discover	Compare	Hypothesize	Discriminate	Opinion
Collect	Explain	Use	Contrast	Design	Conclude	View
Examine	Paraphrase	Compute		Develop	Argue	Observation
Tabulate	Illustrate	Solve		Formulate	Reformulate	
Quote	Compare	Construct		Rewrite	Predict	
		Calculate			Explain	

Source: Adapted from www.schoolnet.ca/grassroots/e/project.centre/shared/HOThink.asp

Read through the words in each column and make a record of your thoughts with regard to the appropriateness and potential use of these trigger words within their various levels. How readily do you feel they fit? For example, 'explain' appears in Level 2, Level 4 and Level 6. Think of an example of how this term could be applied at the various levels; some suggestions are given at the end of this chapter. Remember too that Level 7, Reflection, refers to personal reflection and, therefore, the words appearing in this column must be personified.

Applying Bloom's taxonomy

We regularly use aspects of this hierarchical taxonomy in our everyday speech. In the classroom, however, the range and application is often limited. The following activity illustrates how the full range of Bloom's hierarchy can be used within the context of a well-known nursery rhyme.

Activity 4.3 Bloomin' questions – developing the full range of questions

Each question below illustrates how the different developmental elements of Bloom's taxonomy can be used progressively in a familiar context. Answer the questions and decide which developmental level each question represents.

Humpty Dumpty sat on a wall
Humpty Dumpty had a great fall
All the King's horses and all the King's men
Couldn't put Humpty together again

- Where was Humpty Dumpty sitting before he fell?
- How many of the King's men couldn't put Humpty together again?
- What do you think caused him to fall?
- Think of another nursery rhyme that mentions someone falling over.

- If Humpty Dumpty fell into a pile of snow what might have happened?
- What are the last two lines of the rhyme telling us?
  - How well do you think it does this? Explain your answer.
- How could you make sure that Humpty didn't fall off the wall?

Now apply the approach used in Activity 4.3 to a story, newspaper article or section of text from a book you have recently used in a science session. Use the stimulus questions below to help formulate your own questions: some explanation of the various levels and their usage is given, together with some contextual examples of the higher levels.

Questions for recall – Level 1

- What happened before . . . after . . .?
- How many . . .?
- What is . . .?
- Who was it that . . .?
- How would you explain . . . describe . . . show . . .?
- When . . . why . . . how . . . did?
- Can you identify . . . select . . . picture . . .?
- Who or what were . . .?

Recall-style questions, despite being low order, tend to be the most frequently used form of questioning. As their name implies they are designed to help the pupil recall and revisit ideas and concepts previously covered. They form a useful starting point to the lesson and act as a means of instant formative assessment. The challenge, however, is to ensure that they are not overused and do not begin to dominate our assessment strategies. Some alternative strategies to the continuous use of recall questions are listed in Box 4.2.

Box 4.2 Some alternatives to recall questions

- Use a two-minute, self or peer-marked test

- Try a piece of cloze material as described in Chapter 3, Box 3.1

- Have key points from last session written in advance on the board/ OHP/whiteboard and ask pupils to rehearse the key points with their neighbour, and then go through them briefly

- Make use of a handout with key ideas summarized

- Use bullet points one and two above but build in the occasional error and ask the pupils to 'spot the deliberate mistake'

- Add any ideas of your own

Questions for comprehension – Level 2

Partly set in the context of the Humpty Dumpty nursery rhyme, but also in another well-known context, consider the following comprehension-style questions:

- How would you tell the story of Humpty Dumpty in your own words?

- How do we know what shape and size Humpty Dumpty was?

- How would you explain the problem faced by the King's men?

- What do you think could happen next?

Switching context, think about the story of Jack and Jill going up the hill to collect some water. Jack fell and broke his 'crown'.

- Within this context, can you clarify what the term 'crown' means?

- What example(s) can you give of other nursery rhymes, fairy-tales or stories where things fall down?

- In one of these examples, how can you explain the events leading up to the 'fall'?

Be careful when using questions for comprehension, it is easy to fall into the trap of reducing this style of question to a lower order by asking closed questions, which seek only a yes or no answer; for example, from Activity 4.3 a closed question might be: '*Can you explain why Humpty Dumpty fell?*';

likewise, the developmental level of the questions would be lowered by only seeking answers that repeat information already given. For example, a lower-order comprehension question might enquire how *the rhyme* suggests Humpty Dumpty came off the wall. The answer would '*he had a great fall*' or '*he fell*'; either would be correct but then the question is merely testing the pupil's skill of searching out answers directly from the text. They are essentially factual recall questions. Comprehension, as the term suggests, requires some demonstration of 'deeper understanding', thereby necessitating thought and information assimilation to answer correctly. An example would be to ask what might have caused Humpty to have a great fall. He may have slipped and lost his balance; there are tremendous opportunities here for discussing balanced and unbalanced forces. There again, there is always the possibility that he was pushed! If he was pushed, who might have done it?

This of course makes the whole scenario conspiratorial and raises the levels of interest considerably, at the same time, increasing opportunities for higher levels of challenge!

Questions for application – Level 3

Being able to apply what you know to a novel and ideally unrelated situation gives a sound indication of the depth of your understanding of that concept or phenomenon. The following questions are all examples of application set within a now familiar context:

- Why is Humpty Dumpty falling from the wall an example of unbalanced forces?
- What examples can you find to demonstrate balanced forces?
- Can you group by characteristics such as balanced and unbalanced forces?
- In terms of balanced and unbalanced forces, how would you explain what is happening to Humpty Dumpty and why?
- Do you know of another instance where an unbalanced force makes something move?
- Which factors would you change if you wanted to prevent Humpty Dumpty from falling off the wall?
- Under what circumstances would a parachute help break Humpty Dumpty's fall?
- From the information given, can you develop a set of instructions about sitting safely on a wall?

Application questions play an important role in formative assessment because they serve as a means by which the teacher can assess not only what the pupil 'knows' and is able to reproduce or copy but, more fundamentally, what the pupil really 'understands' about the information in question. This has been referred to as avoiding 'Long John Silver's parrot' syndrome (after Kerry, 2002): like other parrots of its kind, Long John Silver's repeated many key phrases but understood the meaning of very few, if any. We often experience this in our classes and it is for this reason that questions of application are so important. They are invariably 'open'-style questions that encourage the pupil to take existing information, analyse and assess it and then apply it to a new situation. Differentiation can be introduced through the nature of the new situation, be it familiar or unfamiliar; similar or merely related. Application provides opportunities to set scientific concepts within a 'real-life' context; something that is purported widely as being significant to pupil learning and conceptual development.

Questions for analysis – Level 4

Analytical questions are a gift to science education. It is through the analysis of evidence that we tease out the patterns and anomalies, systems and processes that are used to formulate ideas and from them scientific understanding develops. Set within the context of a science investigation, the following questions illustrate analysis on a variety of levels.

A Year 6 class was carrying out an investigation entitled '*Something to mop up with*'. There had been a liquid spillage and, working in small groups, they were charged with investigating a range of materials to determine which would be most appropriate to mop up the mess.

- What was the purpose of using the same type and amount of liquid on the different materials tested?
- How do you know if the approach used is reliable?
- Is the approach used valid? Explain your answer
- If you used syrup instead of water, what might the outcome have been?
- When considering the evidence collected, what was fact and what was based on opinion?
  - o Taking this idea further, what is important information and what is irrelevant?

- What evidence can you find to suggest that kitchen roll is more absorbent than toilet paper?

  o How can you explain this?

Questions of analysis significantly raise the stakes in terms of cognitive challenge. By their nature they encourage the learner to delve deeper into the information and invariably involve some element of subjectivity on the part of the learner. The learner must, however, be able to justify their ideas and this process alone is challenging. Kerry (2002) proposes a step-by-step breakdown of the thought processes involved in answering questions of analysis, stating that the learner must take ownership of the problem before any analytical sense can be made of it. The suggested steps involve:

- breaking down the subject into parts;
- reflecting upon the nature of these parts;
- studying the interrelationships between the parts.

Having successfully achieved these, the learner will have undergone significant intellectual challenge. Once again differentiation can be introduced through familiarity and the nature of the context, and through the degree of support and guidance given. Revisit the analytical questions presented above and decide which ones are associated with the different steps Kerry outlines.

Questions for synthesis – Level 5

The idea of building something new using information acquired elsewhere takes the notion of application into another dimension. Questions of synthesis do this task extremely well if they are worded properly and well thought through. The following examples relate to the outcomes of an investigation to determine which ball will bounce the highest.

- What theory can you come up with for why the 'super ball' bounced the highest?
- What new and unusual uses can you think of for the 'super ball'?
- All the different balls involved in the investigation were designed for a specific purpose; that is football, tennis ball, golf ball, ping pong ball, squash ball and Super Ball.

  o How would you explain the difference in design of the various balls?

- o Suppose you could design your own ball what would it be used for and what would you do?
- What would be a possible solution to . . .?
- Squash balls are more bouncy when they are warm; how could you design/invent a new way to make squash balls bouncy?
  - o What outcome could you predict if this design was applied to all the balls you tested?

When considering questions of synthesis, do not be limited to science concepts and contexts alone; the beauty of questions of this nature is that they can be cross-curricular; that is, skills and practices developed in other areas of the curriculum can be used in a scientific context. Initially this will be limited by your knowledge of the other curricular areas, which is generally not a problem in the primary classroom. One of the benefits of teaching across the curriculum is that you know what the pupils have been taught in the various subject areas. In secondary education subject disciplines are often atomized and establishing links becomes increasingly challenging as subjects become more specialized. So make use of the cross-curricular knowledge that you have and encourage interdisciplinary links through the use of questions of synthesis. An example of this approach to teaching is illustrated in Cinderella's slippers in Chapter 5.

Questions for evaluation – Level 6

According to Bloom's hierarchy the most advanced level of cognitive challenge is that of evaluation. It is debatable as to whether or not this is the case, but the significance of evaluation is its subjective nature. The learner is asked for an opinion on something. Think about the following question-starters in relation to the 'Shopping Bag Game' as described in Chapter 3.

- Is there a better solution to . . .
- Judge the value of . . .? What do you think . . .?
- Can you defend your position about . . .?
- Do you think . . . is a good or bad thing?
- How would you have handled . . .?
- What changes to . . . would you recommend?
- Were they right to do so . . .?

- What are the consequences . . .?
- What would you say is the importance of . . .?
- What are the pros and cons of . . .?
- Why is . . . of value?
- What are the alternatives?
- What would you recommend?

Questions of evaluation by their nature ask pupils to make judgements about something. They are 'open' questions that require the use of evidence and reasoning; often encouraging pupils to compare and contrast with some degree of judgement and rationale (after Kerry, 2002). To achieve this degree of cognition is challenging in its own right, but remember children make judgements from an early age. These judgements are seldom bias-free for they tend to be influenced by commercial advertising and by peers and older siblings. As teachers we must capitalize on such developing skills and nurture them in a pedagogic context. One way to do this is to ask the pupil to justify their answer to this style of question; the answer is often insightful.

Questions for reflection – Level 7

This extension to Bloom's hierarchy takes subjectivity to a different level. Personal reflection asks the learner to step back from the process and examine and critique their performance in the process. Some pupils may find this especially challenging but by careful scaffolding and guidance this fundamental skill of becoming an independent learner can be developed. Consider the following questions from your own perspective, with regard to the type and style of questions introduced throughout this chapter:

- How effective have you been at using a full range of question styles in your teaching?
  - o What evidence do you have to support your answer?
- How much time do you spend in your planning on identifying the questions your will use, or do you tend to make them up as the situation arises?
  - o Do you consider that there is any benefit in pre-preparing a range of key questions to ask during your teaching session?

- How much emphasis do you place on your own evaluation and reflection?
  - Is this done by you alone or discussed with someone else?
  - Do you set targets and recommendations based on this?
- What opportunities do you give your pupils for (a) evaluation and (b) personal reflection?
  - It often helps to share ideas and recommendations arising from such opportunities, so allow the pupils (and indeed yourself) to share these with a 'buddy'.

Promoting independent learning through the use of questions

This chapter began with a question: '*Why is an apple not a fruit, but a tomato is?*'. As you can imagine, this is essentially a terminology issue concerning everyday language and scientific language. In everyday language we refer to an apple as a 'fruit' and a tomato as a 'vegetable'. In botanic terms a fruit refers to a 'fertilized ovary' (nice thought when we consider what we are actually eating, and it is non-meat!). Vegetable, however, is a culinary term and represents any part of the plant that we eat, which is not a fruit. This circular definition requires some explanation of what is meant by a biological fruit and how one gets from the fertilized ovary in a flower to the fruit we find in our fruit bowl. To answer this and the title question requires a degree of anatomical understanding of both the tomato and the apple and how they are formed after fertilization (see Figures 4.1 and 4.2, pages 86 and 87).

A brief lesson in botany

As with animals, the egg or ovum of a plant must be fertilized by the male sex cell. In flowering plants such as the apple and tomato, this takes place within a specialized ovary. Once fertilization has taken place the plant prepares to accommodate the developing embryo and ensure effective dispersal of the resulting seed. In the tomato, a 'true fruit', the walls of the ovary absorb water, becoming fleshy and sweet. The remainder of the flower disintegrates: its job done. Upon ripening the 'fruit' develops a red coloration, attracting animals to ensure dispersal of the seeds.

This sequence of events is periodically interpreted and manipulated by us at all stages of development as we seek the perfect tomato for human consumption. Seed dispersal, the ultimate function of the tomato, is seldom achieved because we eat and digest the seeds. In the wild, however, these seeds would pass through the gut of an animal and be deposited with their own supply of fertilizer enabling germination and growth under appropriate conditions.

So if a tomato is a fruit, why isn't the apple? The same mechanism applies but the difference lies in the detail. In the apple, and indeed other *pommes* such as pears and crab apples, the fleshy part that we eat is not swollen ovary tissue (that may be encouraging to know!): it is 'receptacle' tissue.

By comparing Figure 4.1 with 4.2 you will notice that the receptacle is in the same position in both flowers; it attaches the flower to the flower stalk. In the generalized diagram representing the tomato, you can see that the flower and the ovary are positioned above the receptacle, whereas in the apple the ovary is held *within* the receptacle and the petals of the flower are above the receptacle. The apple or 'fruit' develops from the receptacle and the walls of the ovary remain hard and not fleshy. This is the core containing the pips that we generally discard. The apple 'fruit' also develops upside down. What evidence do we have from the apple itself that this is indeed the case?

Carry out the next Activity (4.4) to help you answer this and the title question.

Activity 4.4 Apples and tomatoes (I)

In scientific terms why is an apple not classed as a 'true' fruit, but a tomato is?

Approach A

What do you need to know to answer this question? An apple and a tomato (both with the stalk attached) would help.

- Look carefully at both the apple and the tomato and make a life-size drawing of each. Observe and note any differences between the two 'fruits'.

- Try to identify any specific features on the outside first, that is, the foliage at the base of the apple (this is dried petals) and the foliage at the top of the tomato (this is dried sepals). Check the location of these on the generalized flower diagram 4.2.

- ○ What does this tell you about the possible position of the flower in relation to the 'fruit'?
- Compare your drawings of the two 'fruits' with the photographs below.

Photograph 4.1 Tomato

Photograph 4.2 Apple

Photograph 4.3 Developing apple fruits

- Now cut the tomato and the apple open. Carefully observe the contents and draw a life-size illustration of each.

- Compare both drawings with Figures 4.1 and 4.2

- What does this tell you about the position of the ovary in an apple and in a tomato?

- *So, why is a tomato a true fruit and an apple not?*

Figure 4.1 Cross-section of a generalized flower (i.e. the tomato)

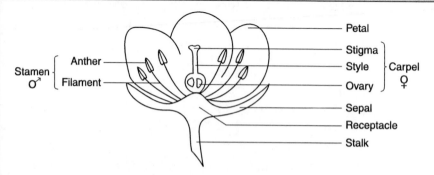

Note: See the developing tomato (ovary tissue) positioned above the sepal and petals. Drawing by L. Lakin.

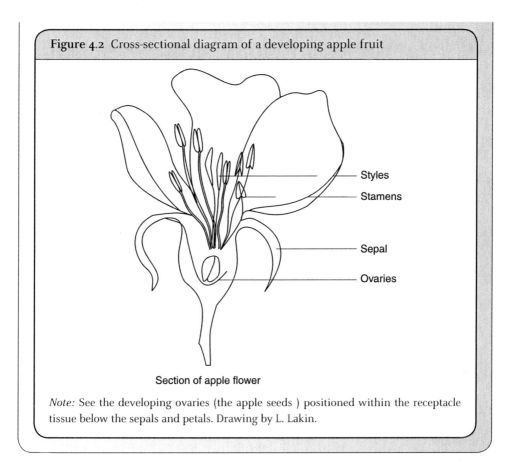

Figure 4.2 Cross-sectional diagram of a developing apple fruit

Styles

Stamens

Sepal

Ovaries

Section of apple flower

Note: See the developing ovaries (the apple seeds) positioned within the receptacle tissue below the sepals and petals. Drawing by L. Lakin.

Having explored the science behind the question, let us pause for a moment and revisit the approach used above from a teaching and learning perspective. Hopefully Activity 4.4 has enabled you to answer the question posed at the beginning of this chapter as to why an apple is not classified as a fruit. You may have understood that the part of the apple we eat is not tissue from a fertilized ovary, but is a receptacle tissue and, therefore, an apple is not classified as a 'true fruit'. A tomato, on the other hand, is. If you did not understand that first time around, perhaps you do now that it has been clarified for you. However, do you really understand the difference or have you just memorized it? This is one of the shortcomings of the activity: it was highly prescriptive and essentially didactic. You, as the learner, were being *told* what to do and answers were readily available from the text. So what have you learnt and retained? You can test this by explaining the difference between an apple and a tomato to someone else later on. To gain a real, in-depth understanding of the idea, you need to take ownership of it. Gaining ownership is part of independent learning, so to achieve this the activity needs amending and the central focus placed on you, the learner (see Activity 4.5).

Activity 4.5 Apples and tomatoes (II)

In scientific terms why is an apple not classed as a 'true' fruit, but a tomato is?

Approach B

Once again you need an apple and a tomato (both with the stalk attached).

- Look at the apple and the tomato closely then do a life-size drawing of each (note why we need to draw them, rather than just looking at them).

- Try to identify any specific features on the outside; that is, the foliage at the base of the apple, the foliage on the top of the tomato; general shape and the position of the stalk – what do they suggest about make-up of the flower before the apple/tomato formed?

- Make a note of one question about the apple and the tomato that you can answer based on your observations (*Note*: This presents an opportunity for differentiation – the higher-level skill of comparison may be too much for some pupils so limit the exercise to either the apple or the tomato initially).

- Now cut the tomato and the apple open. Carefully observe the contents and draw a life-size illustration of each.

- This time, make a note of one question about the apple and one about the tomato that you can answer from your observation *and* your illustration.

- Now make a note of a question that you cannot immediately answer through your observation or your illustration.

- Finally, note three different sources that you could call on to get your answers from.

In order to make a drawing of something directly from observation, you must spend some time examining it. Unfortunately this is something that pupils have increasingly less experience of. Nowadays concentration spans tend to be limited because we have become so attuned to fast-moving stimulation that is a by-product of the technological world we live in. Nonetheless given the opportunity and incentive to sit quietly and observe something can be immensely rewarding: it is a skill, however, that needs to be redeveloped. I say 'redeveloped' because babies and young toddlers do it for much of their waking hours. Translating these observations into a recognizable drawing is a powerful skill. The drawing serves as a vehicle through which our observations are externalizing without the barriers and limitations of the written word.

In Activity 4.5, notice that the learner is doing all the work; they are observing, drawing and even devising questions based on their observations. To achieve this they have to be cognitively engaged. They are even, as the final bullet point requests, identifying a variety of sources from which to obtain answers to those questions they are unable to answer based on their own observation. Possible resources could include:

- *Peers* Pupils need to appreciate that collectively they form a unique and valuable source of information. Admittedly some of that information will be questionable, which is why you need to access the information they are receiving, monitor and where necessary develop or correct it.

- *Existing sources such as books, the internet and other similar secondary sources* Once again these will need monitoring and vetting where necessary.

- Finally they can ask *you*, as the in-house 'expert'. This of course is a potentially scary intrusion. Are you the in-house expert? You may not be and there is no reason why you should be, but there will be someone who is, either within the teaching and support staff or among the parents. It is your role to track down that person and the information. A useful means of accessing an 'expert' within the field is via the science-based Learned Societies that can be contacted via their respective websites (listed at the end of this chapter). By emailing your query to the education contact details on the website, an 'expert' within the field should be able to answer your question. It is definitely worth a try.

Developing independent learners by encouraging pupils to ask questions

Having mastered the skill of communication through language, children continue to make good use of it; incessantly it seems, asking questions and demanding answers that satisfy their increasing curiosity. Unfortunately the pressures of an assessment-led curriculum often challenge this innate enquiring mind, potentially reducing the pupil and the education they receive to mono-directional 'delivery' received by an increasingly passive 'sponge'. How often do we detect the pupil response '... don't teach me, just tell me the right answer'?

The problem with a 'delivery' method of education is that the recipient may not 'pick up' that which is delivered. The problem with the passive 'sponge' reception is that the recipient can only 'absorb' so much. Both processes need to be active, with the pupil taking ownership of and responsibility for the learning process. This theme emanates throughout this book and, as we have seen, comes to the fore through questioning.

Reformulation and reflection

By the very nature of your job, as a teacher you are continuously presented with opportunities to reformulate your ideas and understanding. As a primary school teacher you teach across the subject disciplines and invariably outside your specialist area. You may be self-taught in some subjects, developing your own conceptual understanding as you teach the subject. In secondary science education you may also find yourself teaching outside your preferred subject discipline, having to brush-up on aspects of physics, chemistry or biology that you were not too familiar with. It is often said that you know if you understand something when you can teach it effectively to someone else. How often though do we stop and question our own understanding and our own interpretation of the information we teach? Unless we take time to truly reflect on our practice we will never know whether or not we are fully cognizant and in command of the relevant facts and information, while understanding the concept and the context they are applied to. Take time to try the next activity that focuses on progression within the subject area you are teaching (see Table 4.2). Remember the features of progression in pupils' learning as you work through Activity 4.6(a).

Table 4.2 Features of progression in pupils' learning in science		
From	→	**To**
Simple	→	Complex
Concrete	→	Abstract
Describing phenomena	→	Explaining phenomena
Everyday language	→	Scientific language
Teacher dependent	→	Teacher independent
Unstructured exploration	→	Systematic investigation
Simple representation	→	Conventional representation

Source: Adapted from Annex E: DfEE Circular 4/98 (1998). See also Annex H: DfEE Circular 4/98 (1998)

Activity 4.6(a) is one of reflection and it relates to an aspect of science that you taught recently and perhaps found more challenging than other aspects of science.

Activity 4.6(a) Reflective practice (I)

This activity is in two parts, Part (a) examines a particular aspect of science that you recently taught in terms of conceptual progression within the broader scheme of work for that conceptual area. Part (b) asks you to reflect upon your practice in terms of pedagogic progression, conceptual development and pupil learning. So we begin with a contextual analysis of your taught session.

Answer the following questions:

- Which area of science are you going to analyse and why do you find this more challenging than other areas?

- Identify one particular taught session on this area of science and identify the conceptual starting point. For example, if it was a session on materials you may have been exploring the relationship between volume and density; the conceptual area you are working within is 'density'.

○ The conceptual starting point for your session may have been ordering everyday objects by size and shape.

- From this starting point map out the learning journey from lesson start to lesson end point.

- Now consider the broader scheme of work in science for this particular concept area; for example, see the *Density Pyramid* in Chapter 1: Fig 1.1.

- Identify where your teaching session fits within the broader scheme; that is, what will the pupils progress to? In the density example the next stage would be to explore the relationship between volume and mass by controlling one of these variables; that is, either mass or volume.

  ○ What was the preceding stage in the density example?
  ○ What is the preceding stage in the conceptual area you are exploring?

Setting your teaching within the broader conceptual scheme is an important element of teaching and learning. How often do we find ourselves teaching a topic 'out of context' because it is on the current syllabus or annual scheme of work? Owing to the spiralling nature of the science curriculum key concepts and ideas in science have been visited and will be revisited over the longitudinal education curriculum. It is important for both teachers and pupils to appreciate where and how the current taught session fits within the 'bigger learning picture'. By looking back and projecting forward you can set your teaching within this broader context. You will be better prepared to ensure your pupils make progress rather than merely repeat activities and learning that potentially stifles their conceptual development.

Activity 4.6(b) challenges you to think again in terms of progression and pupil learning and to consider where the opportunities were for pupils to reflect back to previous learning, setting the present within the broader context of conceptual development.

Activity 4.6(b) Reflective practice (II)

Having set your particular aspect of science within the broader context of progressional development for that conceptual area, now consider your practice within these terms. Have a go at the following questions:

- When you plan your taught sessions, how much attention do you give to when and how that concept was taught before?
  - o How do you find out what the pupils know and understand about this area before you plan your session?
- When you plan your session how much attention do you give to where the conceptual understanding will lead; that is, what progressional routes are available to the pupils in the next stages of their development?
  - o What opportunities for progression were apparent in your taught session?
  - o Identify the nature of these opportunities and how they relate to conceptual development.
- With regard to your own understanding of the concept concerned, how aware are you of the various developmental stages?
  - o What questions do you need to ask to explore your own understanding and interpretation to allow you to build a progression chart for the concept you are exploring?
  - o What questions will you ask of your pupils to enable you to ascertain their stages of development within this progression?

There are some searching and demanding questions posed within this activity, so what have you as a learner learnt from this exercise and how can you apply this learning to the next area of conceptual development you teach? The answer to this will be predicated by your own knowledge and understanding both conceptually and professionally. As the above activities suggest, by breaking down conceptual areas into developmental 'chunks', a picture of progression is created that will help both you and your pupils' development and ultimately set learning within the wider context.

The exercise you have just performed served two purposes: one of reflection and one of reformulation. You have re-examined an episode in your teaching and the pupils' learning; placed it under a magnifying glass and analysed the process, the content, the outcome and the potential for development. You have explored your own understanding of the concept and broken it down into manageable 'conceptual chunks'; 'chunks' that allow for progression and consolidation, the process of which can be applied to other situations. From that one exercise, you should have accomplished a great deal. How often do we afford our pupils the same opportunity?

Summary

During this chapter we have considered the role of questioning within the science classroom, explored the type of questions we ask and why, and identified specific strategies for developing and using questioning techniques to assist progression and conceptual development. Pivotal to this process is establishing opportunities for pupil reflection and reformulation thereby encouraging pupils to take ownership of their learning.

As we move into Chapter 5 we explore further this idea of reflection and reformation from the pupil's perspective, by asking the question:

'How can we encourage each pupil in our care to grasp and develop the skills of reflection and reformulation on their journey to becoming independent learners, at the same time satisfying the demands and pressures of the modern-day classroom?'

Suggestions from Table 4.1 Bloom's taxonomy

The following examples are all set within the context of an investigation into the affect of surface on the 'bounciness' of balls. They demonstrate how the term 'explain' can be used to assess various levels of cognitive progression.

- Level 2 Comprehension – 'Explain/describe which surface you think will make the ball bounce the highest.' [Prediction]

- Level 4 Analysis – 'Explain why you think the lino made the ball bounce higher than the carpet.' [Comparison]

- Level 6 Evaluate – 'Explain how effective you think the investigation was at testing the bounciness of balls on different surfaces.' [Assessing]

Question types from Activity 4.3

- Where was Humpty Dumpty sitting before he fell? **Recall**
- How many of the King's men couldn't put Humpty together again? **Recall**
- How does the nursery rhyme suggest Humpty Dumpty came off the wall? **Lower-order comprehension**
- What do you think caused him to fall off? **Higher-order comprehension**
- Think of another nursery rhyme that mentions someone falling over? **Application**
- If Humpty Dumpty fell into a pile of snow what might have happened? **Analysis/Application**
- What are the last two lines of the rhyme telling us? **Analysis**
  - How well do you think it does this? Explain your answer. **Evaluation**
- How could you make sure Humpty didn't fall off the wall? **Creating/ Synthesis**

Learned Society website addresses

Association for Science Education: www.ase.org.uk
Institute of Physics: www.iop.org/
Royal Society of Chemistry: www.rsc.org
Society of Biology: www.societyofbiology.org

CHAPTER 5

Enhancing independence, interdependence and the higher-order skills

Fairytales, electricity scramble and going beyond 'Father Christmas'

Introduction

In Chapter I you were asked to consider how you set about learning a new task. The task was deliberately set within the context of extending a previously learnt activity: a new dance routine, a new swimming stroke or using a new computer software package, for example. The intention was that you were familiar with the context you focused on; that is, you may be a keen dancer, swimmer or a computer enthusiast; the *challenge* was to learn something new within that familiar context. The question for this chapter is, 'why is learning something from scratch more difficult than extending learning within an already familiar context?' We often say that pupils of primary age are able to learn new skills and activities more easily than adults. Why is this?

During this chapter I explore this idea within the context of developing learning in primary and early secondary science, while recognizing that part of our role as teachers is to guide and facilitate this process. I also acknowledge the role of peer support and other social influences, hence the term 'interdependent learning'. Encouraging pupils to externalize their ideas and discuss them with others hones and enhances the higher-order skills of 'independent learning' discussed in earlier chapters; throughout this chapter we explore different ways of making this possible.

Included in this process of enhancement is the use and development of higher-order questioning, as introduced and explained in Chapter 4. We apply questioning techniques of critical awareness and evaluation to the learning environment and introduce 'metacognition' (thinking about thinking). Pupils will to be ready to apply these skills and techniques at different times depending on their cognitive developmental stage; some will be ready to do this before others, some possibly not at all. I refer to this as the 'Father Christmas Syndrome': until pupils are ready to cross the concrete/abstract threshold; for example, being *cognitively ready* to challenge the existence of this fictitious festive character, these higher-level skills of critical awareness, evaluation and reflection generally remain beyond reach. From a cognitive perspective there are ways of progressing towards the use and development of higher-order questions and the activities included throughout this chapter aim to do just that. One mechanism for achieving this is the use of 'problem-based' learning. Introduced as a vehicle for promoting 'thinking' as well as 'talking', problem-based learning encourages the externalization of ideas, and can be an effective means of peer and self-assessment. The importance of establishing a 'learning community' is fundamental to this process of interaction and the subsequent progression towards interdependence. Throughout the chapter, opportunities for achieving interdependence within the primary and early secondary classroom are identified and explored. As with earlier chapters, strategies and their associated activities are set within a scientific and/or technological context, always with a strong relevance to 'everyday life'. The chapter concludes by exploring opportunities to encourage young learners to practise and develop independent and interdependent learning, ensuring they are ready to transfer these skills beyond the formal learning environment to less structured, informal opportunities presented through such vehicles as 'out-of-classroom' learning and 'homework'; the latter of which is the focus for Chapter 6.

> **Key ideas in this chapter:** 'Father Christmas Syndrome'; developing learning and thinking skills; metacognition; self and peer assessment; problem-based learning; learning communities; interdependence, how science works.

Learning and the spiralling curriculum

Although the contents of the school curriculum have waxed and waned over the years, a pattern of consistency has been retained since the mid-1990s when the major overhaul of the English National Curriculum took place. That pattern assumes a spiralling of subject knowledge: spiralling ideally in terms of progression, conceptual development and depth of understanding. This has not always been achieved in reality; indeed, we often get faced with the annual chorus from early secondary pupils stating '. . . *we did the universe in primary school*' or top primary pupils, '. . . *we learnt this with Mrs X last year*'; so why the persistence of the spiralling curriculum?

Consider the two scenarios outlined in Box 5.1.

Box 5.1 'Buttons and Liz don't go!'

I am one of those people who find computers and information technology an anathema and a necessary 'challenge' in my job; so much so that I have to force myself to become even marginally proficient at using them. My children, however, take great delight in pointing out my incompetence at the use of something that comes as second nature to them! So why is it that they find using a computer and the latest mobile gadget so easy to manipulate and I throw up my hands in horror?

Sewing and knitting on the other hand is quite another story; I will readily tackle a new pattern or stitch, while my son and daughter struggled unsuccessfully to achieve a knitted square to add to the local charity blanket!

The difference between these two scenarios is that my children, like most young adults today, were brought up in an age when computers were becoming a household and education commodity. They readily played games on the old BBC computer and 'squealed' with delight when a new Macintosh PC crossed the threshold of the family house. Learning to use computers and mobile phones became second nature in their everyday life: skills that were eagerly adapted and developed with each new commodity within their financial grasp. Knitting (it even *sounds* archaic), however, was a completely new concept; both children struggled to master this and gave up reluctantly when the end product seemed fit only for the recycling bag. The problem was that it was a completely new skill alien to anything they had done before. There had never been a need or a motivation for them to develop this skill and when later in life they decided they wanted to 'have a go' they found that their lack of patience, the need for a quick reward and genuine frustration, all contributed towards the rather sad and unproductive outcome.

Perhaps the problem went deeper than merely trying to learn a new skill later in life. Let's face it there are thousands of people undertaking career changes when they are older; all requiring the acquisition and development of new skills. They may take longer to grasp and perfect, but it can be done. Perhaps it has something to do with the *way* the skills are taught as well as the social drivers of motivation, relevance and confidence. Kibble (2006) suggests that the sequence in which concepts within an area of science are taught is fundamentally important to the learning process. Consider Activity 5.1.

Activity 5.1 Electricity scramble

Electricity needs a complete circuit before it flows	You can measure an electric current using an ammeter	A switch will make or break a complete circuit
Most electrical conductors are made of metal	Materials which do not conduct electricity are called insulators	Materials that conduct electricity are conductors
The more bulbs in a series circuit the harder it is for the electricity to pass through	A battery provides a push for the electrons. It gives them energy	In an insulator there are electrons but they are not free to move around
Electrons do not come from the battery. They are already part of the metal in the wires	When a circuit is complete an electric current flows around the circuit	The electric current is the movement of tiny particles called electrons

Source: after Kibble (2006)

Note: The table above lists a set of statements to do with electricity and the process of electrical conduction. Place these statements in a meaningful sequence for learning.

In this activity you had to rearrange the statements to compile a sequence of learning. This could be done in a variety of different ways; one possible solution is illustrated in Table 5.1.

The learning sequence presented above falls neatly into three categories:

- experiential learning – based on 'concrete' ideas;
- theoretical learning – based on 'abstract' ideas;
- theoretical learning – reinforced through experience.

From the terminology used it is evident that there is progression built into the process. As discussed in Chapter 4, progression develops from the experiential to the theoretical; from the concrete to the abstract. These approaches would not be taught at the same time but rather at different

Table 5.1 Electricity scramble – possible learning sequence		
Electricity needs a complete circuit before it flows	Materials that do not conduct electricity are called insulators	The more bulbs in a series circuit the harder it is for the electricity to pass through
A switch will make or break a complete circuit	When a circuit is complete an electric current flows around the circuit	You can measure an electric current using an ammeter
Materials that conduct electricity are conductors	The electric current is the movement of tiny particles called electrons	Electrons do not come from the battery. They are already part of the metal in the wires
Most electrical conductors are made of metal	A battery provides a push for the electrons. It gives them energy	In an insulator there are electrons but they are not free to move around
Experiential learning based on 'concrete' ideas	*Theoretical learning based on 'abstract' ideas*	*Theoretical learning reinforced through experience*

stages throughout the learner's development. Looking back at Table 5.1 you will probably recognize learning sessions carried out with very young pupils, with those in middle primary and those in top primary/early secondary education. The conceptual area, that is, electricity, is the same but a progression in learning and teaching has been built in; this is the essence of the *spiralling curriculum* and is present throughout school curricula.

There are, however, several potential traps associated with this approach that are all too readily manifest: the main one is that *progression* is replaced with *repetition* not only in conceptual terms but also in experiential terms; that is, the same equipment is used each time. Just think how often chocolate and/or water are used to demonstrate changes of state and the rather 'tired' electricity equipment is brought out for the electricity experiments. Depending on what is being taught, real-life scenarios can help refresh and revitalize an overused approach, while bringing in that element of progression. Consider the example of 'forces' illustrated in Case Study 5.1.

Case Study 5.1 Bend it like Beckham

Have you ever wondered why Beckham was able to 'curl' the ball when he kicked it, making him indispensable when it came to taking free kicks, penalties and corners?

With the help of a ping-pong ball, a couple of straws and the information presented below set up an investigation to demonstrate how you could 'Bend it like Beckham'. Remember it is an investigation so:

- What will you change?
- What will you keep the same?
- What will you measure, and
- How will you measure it?

Bend it like Beckham!

Well it is all down to something called the Bernoulli principle! The reason behind why birds and planes can fly and why sailing boats can sail!

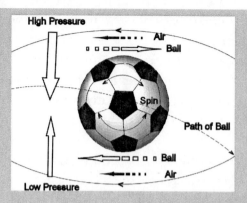

Image by G. Burch

- If the ball is kicked on the left-hand side, this causes the ball to rotate in a clockwise direction.

- The ball side rotates opposite to the airflow (blue line above) around the ball; this increases pressure.

- The right-hand side of the ball rotates in the same direction as the airflow, reducing air pressure.

- This difference in pressure results in the ball being pulled in the direction of the low pressure air, so it curves to the left – so how about that!

Of course an activity like this can become dated very easily, but with some tweaking and updating it can be made topical and interesting for any top primary class. Add the latest football star and set it within the context of the most recent football event, be it Rooney at the Olympics or 'Joe Bloggs' at the local game. For progression and assessment purposes the activity can be developed by challenging the pupils to act as a sports scientist and prepare a training plan for would-be future David Beckhams.

Conceptual change: *the Father Christmas Syndrome* (TFCS)

'The Father Christmas Syndrome' is a cognitive term relating to a pupil's stage in their development regarding the transition from concrete to abstract thinking. Piaget described this development as progressing from the 'concrete' to 'formal' operational thinking (Bennett, 2003). During the former stages, pupils' thinking is based on their experiences of real (i.e. concrete) objects and events. In the formal operational stage pupils are able to deal with abstract ideas; they are able to hypothesize, predict and evaluate by 'standing back' from a situation and analysing it objectively; hence the association with Father Christmas. It is important to mention at this point that there exists a host of pedagogic reasons as to why a pupil may be reluctant to give up the belief in Father Christmas – emotional, social and cultural – all perfectly legitimate reasons. In the context of this book I am not referring to these situations, but from a cognitive developmental process. As individual cognitive development progresses at different rates, it is therefore important as a teacher to be cognizant of this process and support pupils accordingly. If the pupil is not cognitively ready to deal with abstract ideas then the type of opportunities you present them with will be very different to those presented to a pupil capable of working with abstract ideas. The important thing initially is how to seek out this information.

Checking for TFCS: the role of formative assessment

The 'Bend it like Beckham' activity described in Case Study 5.1, as with many such activities, is investigation-based. The associated assessment, that is, the sports scientist scenario and the training session plan, focus on science process skills and the ability to translate the information given into a testable hypothesis (I predict that . . . because . . .) and subsequent investigation with required elements of fair testing. This is ideal if the outcomes of the session are process skills related, but what about pupils' conceptual development and understanding; how can you be sure the time is right for progression and is it achievable?

Threshold concepts

Meyer and Land (2006) made some interesting observations about the misconceptions pupils hold and the pedagogic barriers that exist preventing deep understanding and subsequent cognitive progression in pupils' learning. The existence and persistence of misconceptions were discussed at some length in Chapter 2, but the pedagogic barriers, although related to misconceptions, are different. Barriers to understanding and general accessibility to information are issues across the education spectrum, from the very young to university students; it could be a barrier created through language, be it English as an Additional Language (EAL) issue, or simply the fact that the language level being used is too high and not appropriate to the pupils for whom it is being used. On the other hand, these accessibility barriers could arise because the learner is not at the 'cognitively ready' stage to make sense of the information presented. The Piagetian stages of cognitive development described earlier are a case in point. If a pupil thinks and learns ostensibly through experiential, concrete reasoning, they will be unlikely to succeed in the higher-level question posed in the section above. To ascertain the perceived benefits from being able to swerve the ball demands a degree of abstract projection; the pupils must be able to extrapolate mentally to determine what will happen to the ball when it is kicked in such a manner. Unless the pupil has a basic understanding of forces and, more importantly in this situation, is capable of abstract thought and reasoning, they will be unable to tackle this type of question success-fully. It is therefore important for us in a teaching capacity to assess whether pupils can overcome such barriers and are ready to progress to the next stages of cognitive and conceptual progression. This approach to teaching and learning is at the very heart of differentiation. Consider the next Activity (5.2).

Activity 5.2 Goldilocks and the 'just-right' porridge

Having walked through the forest, Goldilocks stumbles on the cottage where the Three Bears live.

She finds three bowls of porridge on the kitchen table:

- One bowl is too hot
- One bowl is too cold, but the third is
- 'Just-right'.

Goldilocks eats some porridge from the third bowl but gets overcome with tiredness before she can finish it. She goes in search of a bed and falls asleep on the 'just-right' bed. When she wakes up, she is still hungry and goes back to the kitchen to eat the rest of the 'just-right' porridge, but it is no longer 'just-right'. It has gone cold!

Your task is to work out how to keep the porridge 'just-right' for Goldilocks while she sleeps.

To help with your task, think about the following questions:

- What do you know?
- What do you need to know?
- How are you going to find out?

- Once you have that information, does it help?
  - If yes, explain why?
  - If no, what do you need to do now?
- Once you are satisfied with the information you have, design and carry out an investigation to keep the porridge 'just-right' for a set period of time.
  - You will need to consider what you will change.
  - What you will keep the same, and what will be controlled?
  - How and what will you measure?
  - How will you record your results?
- Having completed your investigation, take a few minutes to consider whether or not the information you have is fit for purpose. Does it answer how to keep the porridge 'just-right' for Goldilocks?
  - If not, what would you have to do to make sure that your investigation did answer the question?

The activity described in Activity 5.2 is one of problem-solving; the pupils are given a task and together in a small working group, they set about solving the problem. Having solved the problem, they then have to communicate their solution through some means of communication:

- a role play or other means of verbal presentation;
- a Power Point presentation;
- poster, cartoon strip, story pages, newspaper article, technical journal/ operating manual, and so on.

What places this activity aside from other problem-solving activities are the scaffolding questions at the end. Consider how your pupils tackle a problem-solving task. Experience suggests that they go 'straight for the kill'; one person usually has an idea or has tackled a similar problem in the past and then proceeds to monopolize the group, just short of dictating who should do what, when and how. Does this sound familiar? If it does, the scaffolding questions may help. The group of pupils spend some time analysing the information, teasing out what they already know from this and from any other source immediately available; that is, themselves! The value of this last suggestion does depend on the nature of the task in hand, but remember, each pupil brings their own experiences and ideas to the problem and they should all be encouraged to do so. You may feel that structuring this stage of the activity even more may be necessary; do the pupils need to appoint or have appointed a 'chairperson' and 'scribe' – how does their role allow them to contribute to the discussion? This and other issues of group dynamics will need to be explored and a decision made by you before the activity is set.

The next step is for the pupils to critically analyse the accumulated information that they have teased out, drawing out gaps in their knowledge, which will need to be filled before they can move on. For example, they will need to decide what 'just right' actually means to Goldilocks; is it a specific temperature? At this point you may need to give the pupils a temperature to work to if they have not decided upon one of their own or if theirs is impractical within the classroom setting. From these discussions the pupils move on to design and undertake an investigation to ensure the porridge can be maintained at a certain temperature. The investigation would need to adhere to all the necessary requirements of a fair test but further to this, the pupils are asked to consider the validity of the test, that is, does it give them the information they need to answer the investigating question? All too often this is unfortunately not the case!

The benefits of this detailed and supportive approach to problem-solving, through encouraging the pupils to develop and practise those higher-level skills of critical analysis, are reflective evaluation and procedural planning; skills that are fundamental to independent learning.

Fine-tuning higher-order thinking skills: metacognition, reflection and creativity

From the learner's perspective the ability to reflect upon one's own learning has become widely recognized within teaching and learning (Maiteny, 2002; Pollard, 2002; Ward and McCotter, 2004; Lakin, 2005). The effectiveness of this process, however, appears to depend on the level of reflection administered. A pupil of 7 or 8 years old can reflect upon their own level of knowledge and understanding and possibly suggest in simple terms what they would need to do to progress to the next level of attainment. Likewise a pupil at lower secondary level (about 12 or 14 years old); but at what stage does this cease being the superficial 'explain something rather than describe it' from the more detailed progression leading to conceptual change whereby their understanding deepens and they are able to apply that knowledge? To achieve conceptual change, with or without the input of a teacher, the learner (as emphasized through the early chapters of this book) needs to be actively engaged in the learning process. Pupils must be given autonomy over organization of the learning and to achieve this they will need to engage in thinking! But don't we do that all the time? How often though do we tell our pupils to '. . . think about what they are doing'? So, what do we understand by 'thinking' and how can it be effective?

Activity 5.3 Thinking skills

Discuss the following questions with a colleague at work:

- Do you consider 'thinking' to be a higher-order activity?
- Is 'thinking' a skill that can be taught and, therefore, learnt, and if so, can it be broken down into progressional steps?
- Is thinking context dependent?
  - For example, does it have to relate to a specific scenario or situation?
- How could you promote and develop 'thinking-centred' learning?

Although the questions in Activity 5.3 might fuel some debate, as a species we are not referred to as *Homo sapiens* – thinking man – for nothing! The ability to think is innate but the capacity to use our power of thought in the ways described in this book has generally been learnt, developed and practised. For the learning process to be productive, time is required for the learner to reformulate the ideas they are inputting, to assimilate them and take ownership of them. Until this happens the learner's engagement is only superficial, and deep learning (the acquisition of higher-order skills such as analysing, interpreting and evaluating information rather than simply amassing, reproducing and describing it) is not achieved (Hill and Woodland, 2002).

As mentioned earlier in Activity 5.2, part of this developmental process is to recognize and fill in the information gaps. These often relate to misconceptions in subject knowledge and understanding. If the learner has the ability to tease out knowledge and, with help, present it progressionally, they can identify and recognize stages in the development of a concept. In Chapter 1 and later in Chapter 3 reference is made to progressional development in a pupil's understanding of density, for example. This approach can be applied to any conceptual area in science. Take photosynthesis for example. What pedagogic stages would a pupil need to go through to progress from understanding that a green plant requires sunlight, 'air' and water to grow, to understanding, and later explaining, that it is a combination of carbon dioxide and water that is needed, along with the other requirements, for a plant to grow? See Box 5.2 for some suggestions:

Box 5.2 Progressional development in photosynthesis

At lower primary pupils are taught that plants need light and water to grow. This often involves the 'cress experiment' where cress seeds are put in different conditions to see if they 'grow'. Unfortunately this experiment is flawed from this point onwards for two main reasons:

1 Seeds do not grow initially, they germinate. Germination has very different requirements to plant growth.

2 Germinating seeds seldom require light to grow; they should be kept in the dark but, like seedlings, they do need water to grow.

Hence the desired outcome of the experiment, which is that plants require light and water for growth, is true but not for seeds.

As pupils' knowledge of plant growth develops, they soon realize that a warm temperature (associated with light usually) and air are also required. The next step is to appreciate what fuels the growth and this is where pupils get confused about plants and the need for food. They are fully aware that plants have roots and these are in the soil.

The next cognitive leap is that plants do not get their food from the soil. Agreed, they get nutrients from the soil water but they manufacture their own food using a combination of sunlight energy, carbon dioxide and water, catalysed by the green pigment, chlorophyll in their leaves.

This is a huge cognitive leap which, together with the fact that plants also respire all the time thereby generating their own carbon dioxide for photosynthesis, causes many early secondary school pupils a great deal of confusion. So what can be done? Analogies and role play are both tried and tested solutions; the first working particularly well when you consider the similarity between humans taking multivitamins or other supplements and 'feeding' plants with Baby Bio or other such fertilizer product. In neither case are the supplements a replacement for food.

Getting to grips with photosynthesis

So, plants manufacture their own food – a difficult concept that requires some basic understanding of chemistry as well as the components of a balanced diet; that is, carbohydrates, proteins, fats and vitamins. The fact that the vast majority of plants are green suggests that this may have something to do with their survival and giving the substance that makes plants green a special name, chlorophyll, completes that aspect of the story. Essentially, however, that is what it is, an abstract story that needs personalizing so that the pupils can go some way to understanding the concept. One class of 11 and 12-year-olds developed a role play activity depicting the photosynthetic process using a series of 'character cards' directing the activities. Assisted by their teacher they acted out the passage of water up the stem of a giant plant drawn on the tarmac in the playground. Some pupils represented packets or photons of light and came bouncing into the green leaves, causing the water to give up its oxygen to the atmosphere. Pupils representing water had either the word 'oxygen' written on the back of their card or 'hydrogen'. The newly released oxygen went searching for a partner and duly disappeared into the atmosphere through little gaps in the leaves. The hydrogen, however, needed to track down a carbon dioxide molecule. This was the final character to contribute to the story – carbon dioxide molecules came flooding in through the leaves. When they found some hydrogen atoms inside the plant they joined forces and became a carbohydrate; the end product of photosynthesis but the starter chemical for building the other dietary requirements such as proteins and fats.

Having carried out such a role play activity as described in Box 5.2, the important next step is to ensure the pupils revisit the ideas they enacted, assimilating the ideas and reconstructing the process. This can be done verbally or in the form of a written exercise. However it is performed, it is important to ensure that this process of reformulation takes place. The teacher can identify any misconceptions and gaps in the process and the pupil is continuously reinforcing and building on their understanding. However, as with all these ideas and suggested activities, as a teacher you must be comfortable that the environment in which your pupils are working is non-threatening and conducive to this type of constructive creativity. For it to be most effective and for the pupils to build strong, collegiate working relationships in the classroom, a learning community needs to be established. It is on the development of this classroom community that the rest of this chapter focuses.

Learning communities and developing interdependence

The importance of a learning community, one that supports and enables its members through the learning process, has been widely recognized across the education spectrum. Such communities can exist within a classroom; across classes; and between schools both locally and geographically removed. The important thing to remember is that membership of such a community is determined by the activity being undertaken; only those people involved in the activity in hand assume membership of that particular community. Dabell (2003) suggests a variety of ways of creating a family community within your own classroom:

- Working as teams and in smaller groups to promote partnerships and interdependent behaviour.
- Developing classroom structures that develop individual and group problem-solving, similar to the activities already discussed in this chapter.
- Encouraging a co-operative atmosphere, playing down the more competitive elements, but recognizing that healthy competition in a non-threatening manner is a bonus. To achieve this type of competition everyone must be encouraged and given the opportunity to play to their strengths. Creativity and careful planning on the part of the teacher can enable this type of scenario.

Dabell and others recognize that general group dynamics will invariably apply in any group work situation, but for learning and the community to be effective each pupil and their comments must feel valued. This is perhaps one of the biggest barriers to learning in a group or community situation. There needs to be a leader – an organizer who manages the operation – likewise designers and developers, scribes and 'technicians'. Some members and indeed groups generally fall easily into the role, while others fall to pieces even before they have started! Wegerif (2003) explains the importance of self-imposed ground rules, established and signed up to by each member of the group and community. He goes on to describe a lesson on talking with 11- and 12-year-olds where the pupils are presented with a list of 'talk words', for example: argument, challenge, discussion, reason, and so on. In small groups the pupils, having been issued with a dictionary and thesaurus, research and agree a meaning for the words. In a second activity, they move on to agreeing six important rules that people should follow when talking in groups. As a class, skilfully guided by their teacher, they agree a set of ground rules suitable for generating exploratory talk; Box 5.3 illustrates such a set.

Box 5.3 Our talking rules

- We share ideas and listen to each other
- We talk one at a time
- We respect each other's opinions
- We give reasons to explain our ideas
- If we disagree we explain why we disagree
- We try to reach some agreement in the end
  - This may mean revisiting our original idea.

Source: Adapted from Wegerif (2003)

Ground rules are essentially support mechanisms enabling groups to try to rise above the barriers of group dynamics. To achieve this takes time and trust on all parts; something worth striving for in the classroom. Other support mechanisms worth putting in place aim to help those pupils who struggle or, indeed, those who need further challenges. With appropriate planning and careful monitoring pupils themselves can offer this type of support and/or challenge, as illustrated in Case Study 5.2.

Case Study 5.2 Cinderella's slipper

The story of Cinderella forms the backdrop to this activity and the plenary that follows. During a technology session 10 and 11-year-old pupils designed and made Cinderella's slipper. The activity was divided into various tasks with all pupils carrying out each stage.

Prompted by the table below, pupils were asked to reflect on and evaluate how well they felt they performed each task. It is this information that formed the support mechanism within the classroom. If a pupil decided they were good at fixing the 'toe part of the slipper to the sole' for example, they could be encouraged to explain what they did and how they did it, offering help to those who struggled with that element of the activity.

Task	Expert ☺	Bit dodgy ☺	Need help! ☹
Designing the slipper			
Attaching the toe			
Decorating the slipper			
Attaching the heel			

Monitoring of self-professed expertise is important to ensure the appropriate guidance and support is transferred to others. This type of formative information is invaluable in developing a community of learning that recognizes and builds on pupils' strengths and areas for development without stigmatizing or belittling achievements.

The approach described in Case Study 5.2 has been adapted from an idea developed by a student teacher; the approach could be applied to any science or technology-related set of tasks. As with all formative assessment opportunities, it is how one uses the information gained that is important.

Activity 5.4(a)   The learning community

Thinking about communities of learning (1)

Identify at least three different situations when you have had to work collaboratively in a learning environment.

- How did you feel when having to work as part of a team?
  - Explain your answer as best you can.
- Do you feel that you work better in a group situation or individually?
  - Once again, explain your answer.
- What do you consider to be the benefits of working collaboratively?
- What reservations do you have about this approach to learning?

In Activity 5.4(a) you are encouraged to explore your own perception of working collaboratively, possibly with colleagues, with other delegates at a conference or at a similar arrangement where you have been put into groups and asked to work collaboratively on a particular task. It is important to analyse how you felt in this situation; did you feel threatened? Did you feel you worked better when you were able to bounce ideas off others in the group? Was there a maximum number above which you felt uncomfortable? Did you know the other members of the group before the activity commenced, and if so was this a help or a hindrance to effective collaboration?

In Activity 5.4(b) you are asked to use this reflective analysis to inform your thoughts about how you could establish a community of learning in a variety of different scenarios. By discussing these with colleagues you should access a range of views including reservations as well as perceived benefits from such initiatives.

One final example of extending the classroom family and learning community is illustrated in Case Study 5.3 where a secondary school and its main feeder primary schools tackled the problem of transition in a novel and very successful manner.

Activity 5.4(b)   The learning community

Thinking about communities of learning (2)

For this activity you will need to identify a colleague in your own school and one in either a feeder primary or recipient secondary school, depending on the age group you currently teach.

Taking into consideration your answers to Activity 5.4(a) discuss how learning communities could be established in the following situations:

- in your own classroom;
- within the school vertically across the various classes;
- across the feeder primary/recipient secondary arrangements;
- between schools geographically separated; that is, using virtual communication.

Case Study 5.3 Community of learning

Making the move: a 'win-win' situation

Concern had been expressed for several years by this particular school and its feeder primary over the issue of transition from top primary into first year secondary. Every year the new intake into the secondary school lost the best part of the autumn term through induction and transitional issues and unrest. All involved felt the process could be smoother and begin much earlier. At the beginning of the final year in primary school, shortly after the annual Open Evening for prospective pupils, the secondary school embarked on a transition exercise whereby top primary pupils spent one afternoon a week, after school, in the science department, with volunteer pupils from the existing first year. They embarked on Science Club-style activities and investigations, building up strong working relationships that later developed into Crest Award* presentations once the new pupils started at the

* The Crest Awards are a project-based awards scheme for the Science, Technology, Engineering and Maths (STEM) subjects. The projects comprise a series of enrichment activities aimed at inspiring and engaging pupils between the ages of 5 and 19. For more details see the website at www.bristishscienceas-sociation.org/crest-awards.

school the following autumn. Such a scheme not only captured the interest and motivation of the new intake of secondary pupils when they made the transition, but also kept the interest going when they were invited to act as mentors to the new cohort of top primary pupils in the local feeder schools. It was essentially a 'win-win' situation.

Summary

This chapter began by exploring the idea that learning something from scratch was potentially more difficult than extending learning within a familiar context. This idea and its interpretation were then used to explain the philosophy behind the make-up of the 'spiral' curriculum. The role of the teacher and other people, peers and adults within the learning environment was discussed in some depth, recognizing the valuable contribution that discussion and dialogue make to the learning process. The importance of establishing a 'learning community' where all involved feel valued and unthreatened is something to strive for in every learning situation; idealistic maybe, but worth working towards as the benefits for independent learning are enormous. Ways in which this can be achieved by involving parents and guardians through the controversial topic of 'homework' forms the focus of the final chapter.

CHAPTER

6

'... and now for your homework': fishing on your own

Colin Forster

After spending most of the day in school, pupils are typically given additional assignments to be completed at home. This is a rather curious fact when you stop to think about it, but not as curious as the fact that few people ever stop to think about it.

Kohn (2006: 3)

Introduction

This chapter explores the principles of constructivist learning and how it can be applied to science homework for 7-12 year olds, in order to support pupils' development as independent learners of science. We begin by considering the historical political context in which current policy and practice have developed and ask the rather fundamental question about what homework is for. We then explore recent research into the impact of homework in primary and secondary schools on learning, motivation for learning and relationships both within the home and school, before considering how the constructivist theory of learning might be applied to homework practice, drawing on personal research into pencil-free homework and inviting some outside-the-box thinking about how homework practice might be developed to enhance pupils' motivation and skills as independent learners.

Homework is a controversial issue that often raises strong feelings and, sometimes, strong arguments among pupils, parents and teachers. There exists a diverse range of views about its purpose, value and the nature of the tasks. It also takes up a huge amount of time and effort on the part of pupils, teachers and parents, so it is worth asking the rather fundamental question, 'what's it all for?'.

> **Key ideas in this chapter:** Homework; its purpose and history; the application of constructivist principles to science homework activities; activity-based learning and learning-related relationships.

Activity 6.1 The purpose of homework

(a) Try to answer this question with a short and pithy answer:

   What is the purpose of homework?

(b) From your own experience, do you consider homework achieves the purpose you identified in question (a) above?

Where did homework originate from?

There has been a long tradition in secondary schools of setting homework for pupils; however, in primary schools, up until 1988, the picture was much more mixed, with some schools setting regular homework and others being more sporadic in their approach. In 1988, the New Labour government introduced new guidelines for primary schools, designed to establish how regularly primary school pupils should be set homework and how long the pupils should spend on homework each week. The policy set out recommended time allocations for homework that gradually increased for the 10 and 11-year-old pupils doing 30 minutes of homework a day, with a further 20 minutes of reading if the main task was not reading related.

It is important to think critically about how evidence and knowledge are presented, and the following example is a well-known metaphor that emphasizes the need to consider issues carefully. Imagine watching a Sumo wrestling contest. It might be easy to come to the conclusion that Sumo wrestling makes you fat, since all the Sumo wrestlers you have seen were fat. Obviously, on reflection and with a little more knowledge, it would be possible to conclude that there is a correlation between Sumo wrestling and fatness, but it would not be possible to conclude that one definitely caused the other.

On reading the paragraph in Activity 6.2 (below), you may find yourself asking questions about the nature of the research used to inform the claim that homework can make a contribution to pupil progress. You may have wondered how many pupils and parents saw homework as 'a valuable and essential part of school work' and what the other pupils and parents not included in the 'many' thought about homework. Perhaps, most significantly,

117

Activity 6.2 Critical reading

The extract below is the opening paragraph from the 1998 guidance that set out the government's expectations about how homework should be utilized in primary schools. As an independent learner yourself, read the paragraph below and make a note of any critical thoughts that occur to you or questions it raises about the nature of the claims or the way in which they are presented.

> Research over a number of years in this and other countries has shown that homework can make an important contribution to pupils' progress at school. An OFSTED (Office for Standards in Education) Report published in 1995 (Homework in Primary and Secondary Schools, HMSO, London) confirmed that, 'many pupils and their parents saw work done at home as a valuable and essential part of school work....' Also the 1996/97 OFSTED Annual Report noted that homework is important at all stages in a child's education and that, when used properly, it extends the challenge open to the pupil and ensures that teaching time is used to maximum effect. In this country there is evidence that pupils in the highest achieving schools spend more time on learning activities at home than pupils in other schools.
>
> *Source*: DfEE (1998: 3)

you may have wondered if there was a 'fat Sumo wrestler' hidden somewhere in the final sentence: while there may be a correlation, it may not be possible to claim a causal link between time spent on homework and high achievement from this evidence. A more pragmatic and common-sense interpretation might be that the highest achieving schools have a high number of pupils from socio-economically advantaged families who readily conform to the homework regime and who might spend more time on homework because they are high achieving, rather than the other way around.

Perhaps the key phrase is that homework can be effective '*when used properly*' so it is worth considering what potential benefits and drawbacks there are associated with homework.

Activity 6.3 Benefits and limitations of homework

From your own experiences of homework, as a learner, teacher or parent, make a list of what you consider to be the main benefits or problems associated with homework in both primary and secondary school. These might be either short term or long term and related directly or indirectly to learning.

Potential benefits of homework	Potential limitations/ drawbacks of homework

(Some suggestions are included at the end of the chapter.)

As a result of the publication of the guidelines in 1998, homework became more common and more structured in primary schools, but not universally popular amongst pupils, parents and teachers. In fact, many teachers still express some ambivalence about homework in relation to its effectiveness and impact on learning. Research suggests that teachers often find themselves setting homework even when they are not convinced of its effectiveness. Roberts (2009: 14), reporting on an interview with Martin Hughes (cf. Hughes and Greenhough, 2002), reports that many class teachers

> felt under pressure to set homework on particular days, whether or not it fitted with what was going on in lessons. 'The phrase that kept coming up was "homework for homework's sake",' says Hughes. One teacher went as far as describing it as 'a time-consuming monster that provides very little benefit to the kids.'

In the following section, we explore some of the research that throws some light on the potential benefits and limitations of homework in the primary phase.

Research: homework and the impact on learning, enthusiasm for learning and relationships

Learning

A number of meta-analysis studies (Cooper, 1989; Bonyun, 1992; Sharp *et al.*, 2001) suggest that there is a strong correlation between time spent on homework and pupil achievement among secondary school pupils and

119

it seems that these results may have influenced the way that policy on homework in both secondary and primary schools has been formed.

However, research into the educational value of homework in the primary years is inconclusive (Hughes and Greenhough, 2002). One of the reasons for this is that there have not been many studies into homework in primary schools, particularly in English schools, but even those studies that have been carried out have not revealed any compelling evidence to support the view that a secondary-style homework regime is effective for younger pupils. In a study in the United States of America, Cooper (1989) concluded that homework had a 'negligible impact' or 'non-significant effects' in the elementary school. Where the effects were noted to be significant they were considerably smaller than the effects seen in high school studies.

Activity 6.4 Impact of homework on learning

Identify and list some possible reasons for homework having a limited impact on learning and progress in primary schools as compared to secondary schools.

(Some suggestions are included at the end of the chapter.)

Enthusiasm for learning

Some research suggests that primary age pupils value homework, with OFSTED claiming that their survey found that 'most pupils accepted and even enjoyed homework' (DfEE, 1998: 32). However, this is not a universally accepted view, and an alternative is perhaps best expressed by Kohn (2006: 17): 'Most kids hate homework. They dread it, groan about it, put off doing it as long as possible.' While this is clearly a polarized view, if this is even partly true, then it is unlikely that homework has a generally positive effect on many pupils' enthusiasm for learning. In my own research, I found this to be true, with most pupils claiming not to enjoy homework and parents reporting that their pupils were not enthusiastic about it, such as this parent of 10-year-old pupil:

> 'We do get a bit of a sulky face when I say "Where's your homework?" When he wants to be outside playing with his friends and I'm making him sit down and do what he doesn't want to do, it doesn't make for a great atmosphere, does it, at home?'

Perhaps one of the reasons that pupils are generally not keen on homework is, as Kohn suggests, that they are not completely sure about the purpose of it. Pupils do not see homework as a learning opportunity, but more as something that has to be done and can then be 'ticked off': 'As a rule, the point of homework generally isn't to learn, much less to derive real pleasure from learning. It's something to be finished' (Kohn 2006: 17) In my own research, it became clear that pupils' main motivation for completing homework tasks was so that they avoided being punished at school by submitting their work on time.

Relationships in the home

Lacina-Gifford and Gifford (2004: 279) claim 'almost half of parents reported having a serious argument with their pupils over homework'. In my own research, I found this to be about right with most families reporting that homework was often a site of tension between parents and their pupils. One 11-year-old boy gave this wonderfully vivid example of how a conversation about homework might escalate:

> 'Mum says "you're doing it and that's final" and I say "But what if I don't want to do it right now?" and then Dad will get involved and he'll start shouting and stuff. You'll have mum out in the garden doing something she wants to do, and dad will be sat watching the rugby in a sulk, and I'll be in my room playing on the Playstation.'
>
> *11-year-old boy*

Some of the tension arises from parents trying their best to support their children but finding that either what or how their children are being taught is so different to their own experiences that they find it difficult to know how to support them in their learning, as shown in this example of a parent who was bewildered at how his daughter had been taught to solve maths problems:

> 'I teach her the way I was taught, basically. If she comes out and she's got to figure out a sum, I'll show her how to carry the ones and whatever, but they don't do that at school. They have a line or whatever and they do all this. It's beyond me.'
>
> *Parent of 9-year-old pupil*

Seldom referred to in published research is the impact of homework on pupil-teacher relationships. This is an interesting and important gap in the research knowledge, as it is widely accepted that maintaining a positive, professional and learning-oriented relationship between teachers and learners is essential at every stage of learning. In my own research, I found that the impact of homework on pupil-teacher relationships was an issue identifed by teachers as potentially problematic, as they found themsleves repeatedly nagging the same pupils about non-completion of homework or about the standard of it. However, it was not just teachers who identified some aspects of the potentially damaging impact on pupil-teacher relation-ships, as the example referred to in Activity 6.5 illustrates.

Activity 6.5 Case study 1

The following statement was made by a Year Six pupil during an interview about his experiences of homework. He was talking about his motivation for doing his homework, which was linked to his perception of how teachers might treat you if you have not done it:

> 'They [the teacher] will be helpful but they won't be as [helpful] because they're a bit annoyed with you because you haven't done your homework or brought it in. My friend didn't bring it in and the teacher wasn't helping him. She just said "Write that down." She was still being helpful but not as helpful'.

Reflect on this child's candid insight into teacher-pupil relationships. Could this be just an isolated incident or are there some wider implications for teaching and learning in relation to home-work? Refer back to your responses to Activity 6.3; did you already identify possible impacts on pupil-teacher relationships as a possible issue?

Constructivist homework in science . . . becoming independent and interdependent as a learner

As explored in earlier chapters, current thinking about how pupils learn most effectively in science is best described by the constructivist theory of learning, summarized neatly by Selley (1999: 7):

It is a theory which holds that every learner constructs his or her ideas, as opposed to receiving them, complete and correct, from a teacher or authority source. This construction is an internal, personal and often unconscious process. It consists largely of reinterpreting bits and pieces of knowledge ... to build a satisfactory and coherent picture of the world.

The principles of constructivist learning are well understood and widely accepted in the world of science education. However, as identified in earlier chapters, there is often a mismatch between the beliefs teachers hold about effective learning in science and the learning oportunities they provide for the pupils in their classes. The challenge of setting effective homework is finding ways to take what we know about learning and apply this knowledge to setting effective homework.

So what do we know about effective learning in science? This chapter will reinforce ideas explored in earlier chapters from the perspective of promoting independent learning through the use of homework.

The importance of talk and social interaction and exchange

One of the most well-known proponents of talk in learning is Lev Vygotsky, who suggested that learning is a social process in which what you learn is determined by those around you and that talk between a learner and a 'more able other' is central to the learning process. However, Vygotsky (1962) does not view 'talk' just as a means to learning new facts, but also as a means to facilitating the development of 'higher mental processes'. For example, the ability to plan, evaluate, memorize and reason. Social interactions enables pupils to internalize the intellectual skills needed in order for them to be intelligently independent beings, to be self-regulating and self-developing, by providing a model or blueprint of thought processes, such as how to debate different points of view or evaluate evidence. It is interesting to note, then, that many 'traditional' approaches to homework require pupils to work in a solitary way on a single task; these approaches are applied in the hope that they will develop 'independence' in the pupil, but Vygotsky would argue (and we support this) that they do not provide the social interactions necessary to scaffold the intellectual skills.

The importance of activity-based learning

As discussed in earlier chapters, there is a long-standing acceptance amongst science educators that it is better for pupils to be actively engaged with meaningful investigative and practical activity than to be passive receivers of knowledge. Practical activities enable pupils to engage both physically and cognitively with scientific concepts, and provide opportunities for pupils to take ownership of their learning and raise their own questions. Again, 'traditional' approaches to homework tend to involve writing things on a piece of paper. There are some obvious difficulties associated with trying to get pupils involved in practical activities for their homework, such as ensuring that they have the appropriate resources or space to undertake the tasks. Finding ways around these could be very beneficial to learning.

Creating opportunities for exploring and challenging ideas

In Chapter 3, it was emphasized that the constructivist theory of learning is underpinned by the idea that pupils develop their own scientific thinking in ways that make sense to them; their ideas are sometimes not scientifically 'correct' but are related to the pupils' own experience. They often reveal an intelligent attempt to make sense of the world. Effective learning in science starts with enabling the pupils to understand their own thinking and begin the process of challenging their thinking. Homework tasks are often about reinforcing 'right' answers rather than prompting new ideas or promoting independent thinking.

Ownership and independence

This can be a difficult issue to identify, but it is clear that pupils and adults learn best when they feel there is a purpose to their learning, a relevance that makes it meaningful and worthwhile for them. The challenge in relation to homework is that pupils often feel that it is something that is 'done' to them and in which they see little value or relevance to their lives.

If we aim to support pupils and young people in becoming independent learners, we must remind ourselves what it is we believe makes someone a 'good' learner. Postman and Weingartner (1971), in their seminal text, *Teaching as a Subversive Activity*, provide a useful way of thinking about what good learners believe and do.

Box 6.1 'Teaching as a subversive activity'

First, good learners have confidence in their ability to learn. This does not mean that they are not sometimes frustrated and discouraged. They are, even as are poor learners. But they have a profound faith that they are capable of solving problems, and if they fail at one problem, they are not incapacitated in confronting another.

Good learners tend to *enjoy* solving problems. The process interests them, and they tend to resent people who want to 'help' by giving them the answers.

Good learners seem to know what is relevant to their survival and what is not. They are apt to resent being told that something is 'good for them to know', unless, of course, their crap detector advises them that it *is* good for them to know – in which case, they resent being told anyway.

Good learners, in other words, prefer to rely on their own judgement. They recognize, especially as they get older, that an incredible number of people do not know what they are talking about most of the time. As a consequence, they are suspicious of 'authorities', especially any authority who discourages others from relying on their own judgement.

Activity 6.6 Implications when planning science homework tasks

If we accept Postman and Weingartner's (1971) summary of the characteristics of a good learner, what do you consider are the implications when planning science homework tasks? Make a list of these and discuss them with your colleagues.

Postman and Weingartner (1971: 30; my italic) make the point that '*the critical content of any learning experience is the method or process through which the learning occurs ... It is not what you say to people that counts; it is what you have them do*'. This is sometimes misunderstood as suggesting that practical work is more effective than listening to a teacher; this may be true, but is not the main point of this statement. Postman and Weingartner's main point is that pupils do not learn as much from the content of a learning experience as they do from how that experience is undertaken.

In the case of homework, given everything that we know about learning, we might ask why it is that many homework tasks involve completing a worksheet. Regardless of how well designed or how important its learning content, the hidden messages that pupils might learn through completing dozens of homework worksheets each school year might include:

- learning always involves writing (whether you like writing or not);
- learning that is not written down is not worthwhile;
- learning normally involves repetition;
- learning is normally quite dull;
- learning will only be assessed by a single question: was it handed in on time?

Of course, there are many good reasons for why homework is normally set in a predictable and repetitive manner, with the same kinds of homework set on the same day each week: it is important for pupils to know what is expected of their homework and for parents to know when to expect their pupils to have homework tasks, to know what those tasks will be and when they are due to be handed in; it is also important for the tasks to be manageable for the teacher in relation to setting the task, collecting the work and marking the work. It is worth noting, though, that few of these reasons relate directly to subject-based learning, but more to managing expectations and establishing clear routines.

Approaches to home learning that encourage learning-oriented rather than task-oriented activity

In the previous section, we considered how the principles of constructivist learning are significant in supporting pupils to become effective, independent learners in science. In this section, we explore some approaches to homework that apply these principles to practice and offer some solutions in the quest to make homework a positive and productive learning experience for all pupils.

Activity 6.7 All about learning

Using what we know about learning, design some principles for effective science homework for top primary or lower secondary pupils.

Pencil-free homework

In my own research (Forster, 2011), I explored the use of 'pencil-free' homework tasks, following on from the publication of the 'Active Homework' series (Forster *et al.*, 2010). In pencil-free homework, tasks are set that require pupils to talk to someone at home about a scientific issue, often by undertaking a practical investigation or activity. The homework is 'pencil-free' as there is nothing to write down on the sheet and nothing to hand in to the teacher. The tasks aim to be learning-oriented, through focusing on doing and talking about scientific facts or concepts rather than task-oriented, in which pupils tend to focus on completing the sheet rather than engaging with the learning.

Activity 6.8 Thought experiment

Try this thought experiment, adapted from Forster *et al.* (2010). First, find a friend to talk to about your ideas.

Imagine that you are sky-diving, having just jumped out of an aero-plane; you have not yet opened your parachute. Imagine the wind rushing past, ruffling your clothes and hair and rushing past your face.

Source: David Brookes

Now imagine that all of the air in the world disappears. How will your descent change? What other changes might you notice? What will happen if you open your parachute? What questions do you have as a result of trying this thought experiment?

Activity 6.9 Pencil-free homework

Pencil-free homework might not be the perfect solution to the challenge of setting meaningful science homework. Consider some of the potential benefits and limitations of pencil-free homework.

Potential benefits of pencil-free homework	Potential limitations/drawbacks of pencil-free homework

You set the criteria; now let the pupils set the task

Another approach to consider if you aim to set homework that avoids dull, task-oriented completion of worksheets is to provide pupils with the assessment criteria and give them the choice as to how they demonstrate their scientific understanding or knowledge in relation to the criteria. For example, at lower secondary level, you might set pupils the challenge of demonstrating their knowledge of the parts of an animal cell. The pupils could choose how to do this: some might make a labelled three-dimensional model of an animal cell from modelling clay, while others might make a model using fabrics, and others might produce a labelled diagram. The aim is that, in choosing for themselves how to address the criteria, the learners will engage with the learning more deeply than if they had been set a task over which they had no say and in which they felt no ownership.

Provide a choice of task

This is similar to the previous approach but affords the teacher a little more control over what the pupils might actually undertake in relation to the homework tasks, while still offering the pupils a degree of autonomy over the task. For example, in the topic of 'Life cycle of a flowering plant', pupils in top primary are given a choice of tasks related to seed dispersal:

1 Complete a diagram of the life cycle of a flowering plant.

2 Match pictures of four different seeds to descriptions of the kind of dispersal.

3 Draw a picture/diagram showing three ways in which seed dispersal can occur.

4 Collect a seed from the natural world (without damaging any plants) and decide which method of dispersal applies to this kind of seed.

Projects

The project approach moves away from the setting and submission of short tasks and allows pupils longer to explore a topic and provides them with more choice about how to tackle it. For example, 11 and 12-year-old pupils might be asked to make a PowerPoint, poster or information leaflet on the topic of electricity for a younger audience. The project might involve independent research and independent decisions about how best to present the information to make it relevant and accessible for the target audience.

Collaborative tasks

As emphasized throughout this book, becoming an independent learner is not just about learning to work on your own. A truly independent learner is able to work collaboratively with others and sees this as an important part of the learning process. Collaborative learning enables pupils to engage in both activity and talk with a peer or group of peers to explore and under-stand a topic more deeply. A good product for paired tasks would be a short presentation to the class on a particular topic; preparing a presenta-tion requires pupils to fully understand the topic, to talk it through with each other and to identify the key points to be shared in the presentation. Making the presentation provides a good opportunity for pupils to rein-force their learning through explaining their own understanding to others. However, a note of caution in relation to presentations: try to avoid pupils over-relying on PowerPoint or similar presentation packages; encourage pupils to think through ways to engage their audience using other forms of visual aids such as models, diagrams, pictures or short tasks.

And there are others ....

These are just a few ideas to get you thinking about how to set meaningful and learning-focused science homework for pupils at top primary and lower secondary but you will be able to come up with more of your own. The main challenge is to set tasks that align well with what you believe homework should be for and how best it can achieve these aims (see Activity 6.10).

Activity 6.10 Ideas for effective homework

Based on the outcomes of the activities and explorations in this chapter, identify some new ideas for effective homework. Discuss them with your colleagues and try them out with your class. Remember to ask your pupils what they think about them!

Summary

In this chapter, we have considered the purpose of homework, some of the challenges inherent in setting science homework for pupils in top primary and lower secondary, what we know about learning in science and some possible ways forward to enable homework to create positive and meaningful learning experiences for pupils. In applying this to our own practice, we need to keep in mind what we are trying to achieve with our home-learning tasks and what we are trying to avoid. Science homework has the potential to extend pupils' understanding, develop their ideas and promote their independent thinking and it is these aspects that we want to enhance as we work with pupils to support their development as independent learners.

Some suggestions for Activities 6.3, 6.4, 6.7 and 6.8 are detailed in Tables 6.1–6.4.

Table 6.1 Activity 6.3 suggestions

Potential benefits of homework	Potential limitations/drawbacks of homework
Opportunities to reinforce in-class learning.	It is difficult to set really good homework that reinforces in-class learning and that meets the needs of all children.

(continued overleaf)

Opportunities to provide exciting learning activities to inform and enhance in-class learning.	It is too easy for homework to be boring, and perceived by children as irrelevant and frustrating. It puts some children off learning.
Gets parents involved in the children's learning.	Many parents find that homework is an added pressure in busy family life. Some complete their children's homework.

Table 6.2 Activity 6.4 suggestions

Identify and list some possible reasons for homework having a limited impact on learning and progress in primary schools as compared to secondary schools.

Possibly, secondary school pupils have developed the skills to work more independently and get more out of their homework.

Possibly, secondary school pupils understand the importance of homework and the difference it might make to their grades.

Possibly, the kind of homework that primary school children receive does not impact positively on their learning.

Table 6.3 Activity 6.7 suggestions

Using what we know about learning, design some principles for effective science homework for top primary or lower secondary pupils.

Since talk is central to the learning process, homework tasks should include some opportunities for talk either before, during or after the part of the work done at home. This could be in the form of a discussion with a family member, a paired project, or a mini presentation to the class following some independent research.

Since ownership is important in the learning process, homework tasks should allow for some autonomy (choice) to increase pupils' engagement with the learning. Homework should be varied and interesting.

Since engagement is central to any learning, boring homework should not be allowed. If a thought-provoking or interesting task cannot be found . . . do not set any homework.

Table 6.4 Activity 6.9 suggestions	
Potential benefits of pencil-free homework	**Potential limitations/drawbacks of pencil-free homework**
There is nothing to write down and it is the writing down that for many children turns some interesting learning into a dreary task.	Some children may feel that they have not done anything worthwhile if they have not written it down.
There is nothing to hand in, so the teacher can follow up homework with meaningful discussions instead of marking worksheets.	There is nothing to hand in, so some children will opt out and will not engage.
The doing and talking, both at home and in the follow-up lesson, enhance and reinforce learning.	Some families may not engage in 'doing and talking' tasks.

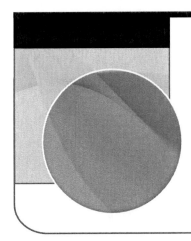

Final summary

This book and the learning journey it described began in Chapter 1 with an exploration of learning and the learning process, with particular emphasis on the importance and relevance of developing independent learners; those who are autonomous and creative in their thinking and constructively critical of their understanding. Chapter 2 introduced a philosophical tenor to the journey by inviting you to consider your perception of science and science education. Developing in parallel with this philosophical tone was a theme of progression and transition and how this might apply to the development from dependent learning to independent autonomous learning. Strategies and activities to enable this progression were discussed and explored in Chapters 3 and 4, and in Chapter 5 the environment within which your pupils learn was scrutinized, with an emphasis on the development of learning communities. These communities were taken beyond the school boundaries in Chapter 6, where the role and use of homework was explored.

Although the focus of this book is on developing independent learners, the learning journey has been about *you* . . .

- You as a teacher: the way you teach and how you engage with your pupils in the learning environment.
- You as a learner: how you learn and then, using the experience and insight into the learning process, how you apply what you have learnt to your teaching.

Having completed this stage of your learning journey and applied where possible the philosophy of this book, you should now be ready to 'fish on your own'. You need to take the information and activities described along this journey and using your professional judgement, your knowledge of your pupils and the environment in which you all work, adapt them, amend them and generally make them your own. That way they will achieve what you want them to, but you do need to be clear about what you want your pupils to achieve from them, and overall you need to be patient; some activities will 'work', others will not! But remember learning is a journey that lasts a lifetime and although you may think that being independent in thought and mind is idealistic, it has become an important necessity in the brave new world we call the twenty-first century.

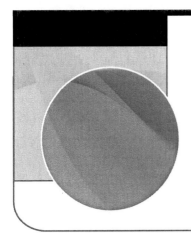

References

Allen, M. (2010) *Misconceptions in Primary Science*. Maidenhead: Open University Press.

Annex E: DfEE Circular 4/98 (1998) *Initial Teacher Training National Curriculum for Primary Science*. London: TTA.

Annex H: DfEE Circular 4/98 (1998) *Initial Teacher Training National Curriculum for Secondary Science*. London: TTA.

Assessment Reform Group (2002) *Assessment for Learning: 10 Principles*. Available from The Institute of Education, University of London and from the ARG website at www.assessment-reform-group.org.

Ausubel, D. (1968) *Educational Psychology: A Cognitive View*. New York: Holt, Rinehart and Winston.

Bennett, J. (2003) *Teaching and Learning in Science: A Guide to Recent Research and its Application*. London: Continuum Studies in Research in Education.

Biggs, J. and Tang, C. (2009) *Teaching for Quality Learning at University*, 2nd edn. Maidenhead: Open University Press.

Black, P. and Wiliam, D. (1998) *Inside the Black Box: Raising Standards Through Classroom Assessment*. London: NFER-Nelson.

Bloom, B. (ed.) (1965) *Taxonomy of Educational Objectives: The Classification of Educational Goals. Vol. 1: Cognitive Domain*. London: Longman.

Bonyun, R. (1992) *Homework: A Review of Reviews of the Literature*. Ottawa: Ottawa Board of Education, Centre for Research, Professional Development, and Evaluation.

Carle, E. (1974) *The Very Hungry Caterpillar*. London: Picture Puffin.

Cooper, H. (1989) Synthesis of research on homework, *Educational Leadership*, 47(3): 85–91.

Dabell, J. (2003) 'Learning and progression: what works?' In *Teaching and Learning: Transforming Education 5–12*, February/March. Milton Keynes: Questions Publishing.

DCSF (Department for Children, Schools and Families) (2007) *National Curriculum Programme of Study for Science*, London. Available online at www.standards.dcfs.gov.uk.

DfEE (Department for Education and Employment) (1998) *Homework: Guidelines for Primary and Secondary Schools.* London: DfEE Publications.

Driver, R. and Bell, B. (1986) Students' thinking and the learning of science: a constructivist view, *School Science Review*, March: 443–57.

Driver, R., Squires, A., Rushworth, P. and Wood-Robinson, V. (1994) *Making Sense of Secondary Science: Research into Children's ideas.* London: Routledge.

Forster, C. (2011) The application of learning theory to homework practice: trialling pencil-free homework in Key Stage Two Science. Unpublished EdD Thesis, University of Gloucestershire.

Forster, C., Parfitt, V., McGowan, A. and Brookes, D. (2010) *Science Homework for Key Stage 2: Activity Based Learning.* London: David Fulton.

Gallimore, R. and Tharp, R. (1990) Teaching mind in society: teaching, schooling, and literature discourse, in L. Moll (ed.) *Vygotsky and Education: Instructional Implications and Applications of Sociohistorical Psychology.* Cambridge: Cambridge University Press.

Hargreaves, E. (2005) Assessment for learning? Thinking outside the (black) box, *Cambride Journal of Education*, 35(2): 213–24.

Harlen, W. (2006) Assessment for learning and assessment of learning, in W. Harlen (ed.) *ASE Guide to Primary Science Education.* Hatfield: ASE.

Harlen, W. (2010) What do studies of the brain tell us about learning? *Education in Science*, 236: 28–9.

Henessey, S. (1998) Teaching composing in the music curriculum, in M. Littledyke and L. Huxford (eds) *Teaching the Primary Curriculum for Constructive Learning.* London: David Fulton.

Hill, J. and Woodland, W. (2002) An evaluation of foreign fieldwork in promoting deep learning: a preliminary investigation, *Assessment and Evaluation in Higher Education*, 27(6): 530–55.

Hughes, M. and Greenhough, P. (2002) *Homework and its Contribution to Learning.* Bristol: University of Bristol.

Kerry, T. (2002) *Explaining and Questioning* (Master Teaching Skills Series). Cheltenham: Nelson Thornes.

Kibble, B. (2006) Progression and continuity, in W. Harlen (ed.) *ASE Guide to Primary Science Education*. Hatfield: ASE.

Kohn, A. (2006) *The Homework Myth*. Philadelphia, PA: Da Capo Press.

Kyriacou, C. (2001) *Effective Teaching in Schools: Theory and Practice*: Cheltenham: Nelson Thornes.

Lacina-Gifford, L.J. and Gifford, R.B. (2004) Putting an end to the battle over homework, *Education*, 125(2): 279–81.

Lakin, L. (2004) The golden age of protein: an initial teacher training perspective on the biological role of proteins in our everyday lives, *International Journal of Consumer Studies*, 28(2): 127–34.

Lakin, L. (2005) Developing innovative pedagogy to enhance teaching and learning in science and environment education, *Forschung und Entwicklungsarbeit*, 5: 397–402, Satz and Drack, Krems, Austria.

Lakin, L. (2010) Independent learning and a paradigm lost, paper presented at The First International Theorising Education Conference, 26 June, University of Stirling.

Lakin, L. (2012) What can I expect my PGCE at M-Level to look like at the subject level?, in K. Sewell, L. Lakin, W. Woodgate-Jones, T. Cain and K. Domaille (eds) *Doing your PGCE at M Level*. London: Sage Publications.

Lakin, L., Lipington, L. and Pask, H. (2004) 'How can science be creative?' *Primary Science Review*, 81: 4–6.

Littledyke, M., Ross, K., Sutton, D., Lakin, L., Shepherd, J., Forster, C., Swann, R. and Mansfield, V. (2003) *Teaching Primary Science*. Gloucester: University of Gloucestershire.

Maiteny, P. (2002) Mind the gap: summary of research exploring 'inner' influences on pro-sustainability learning and behaviour, *Environmental Education Research*, 8(3): 299–306.

Meyer, J. and Land, R. (eds) (2006) *Overcoming Barriers to Student Understanding: Threshold Concepts and Troublesome Knowledge*. Abingdon: RoutledgeFalmer.

Millar, R. (1989) Constructive criticisms, *International Journal of Science Education*, 11: 587–96.

Osborne, J. (1996) Beyond constructivism, *Science Education*, 80(1): 53–82.

Osborne, J. and Dillon, J. (2008) *Science Education in Europe: Critical Reflections*, a report to The Nuffield Foundation, London.

Pollard, A. (2002) *Reflective Teaching: Effective and Evidence-Informed Professional Practice*. London: Continuum.

Postman, N. and Weingartner, C. (1971) *Teaching as a Subversive Activity*. Harmondsworth: Penguin Books Ltd.

Pritchard, A. (2005) *Ways of Learning.* Oxon: David Fulton.

Roberts, C. (2009) 'A benefit – or a burden?' *Professional Teacher,* Autumn: 14–15.

Ross, K., Lakin, L. and Callaghan, P. (2004) *Teaching Secondary Science,* 2nd edn. London: David Fulton.

Ross, K., Lakin, L. and McKechnie, J. (2010) *Teaching Secondary Science: Constructing Meaning and Developing Understanding,* 3rd edn. London: David Fulton.

Selley, N. (1999) *The Art of Constructivist Teaching in the Primary School.* London: David Fulton.

Sharp, C., Keys, W. and Benefield, P. (2001) *Homework: A Review of Recent Research.* Slough: National Foundation for Educational Research.

Thomas, G. (2009) *How to do your Research Project.* London: Sage Publications.

Ward, J. and McCotter, S. (2004) Reflection as a visible outcome for pre-service teachers, *Teaching and Teacher Education,* 20: 243–57.

Wegerif, R. (2003) The importance of intelligent conversations, in *Teaching and Learning: Transforming education 5–12,* February/March. Milton Keynes: Questions Publishing.

Wood, L. (2010) Ricky goes to the Antarctic, *Education in Science,* 238, June.

Vygotsky, L. (1962) *Thought and Language.* Cambridge, MA: The Massachusetts Institute of Technology.

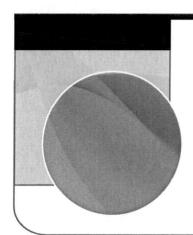

Index

Locators shown in *italics* refer to figures, tables, activities and case studies.